2047-46

Illustrated Treasury

of the

American Locomotive Company

Was This American Locomotive's Most Beautiful in Steam? Rock Island (Chicago, Rock Island and Pacific) 4048 shows the final perfection of USRA styling, with typical USRA lines plus such post-USRA refinements as the cast "Delta" trailing truck under the firebox, cab with canted forward edge (to match the plane of the boiler backhead), tender with faired-in coal bunker.

O. M. KERR

Illustrated Treasury
of the
American Locomotive
Company

Foreword by

H. Stafford Bryant, Jr.

W. W. NORTON & COMPANY

New York · *London*

Printed in the United States of America.

Manufacturing by Halliday Arcata

First Edition.

Library of Congress Cataloging-in-Publication Data

Kerr, O. M.
Illustrated treasury of the American locomotive company / O. M.
Kerr : with a foreword by H. Stafford Bryant, Jr.
p.   cm.
1. Locomotives—United States. 2. American Locomotive Company.
TJ603.2.K48   1990
625.2′6′0973—dc20   90-32551

ISBN 0-393-02599-3
W. W. Norton & Company, Inc., 500 Fifth Avenue, New York, N.Y. 10110
W.W. Norton & Company, Ltd., 37 Great Russell Street, London WC1B 3NU

1 2 3 4 5 6 7 8 9 0

CONTENTS

Foreword: Alco for Enthusiasts

Given the widely varied attitudes of customers and enthusiasts, it may seem unreasonable to rank the great steam locomotive builders of the first part of this century. Ranking would be difficult in all categories: mechanical innovation, business acumen, aesthetic quality of the completed locomotive. American Locomotive Company ("Alco"), the Baldwin Locomotive Works, and the Lima Locomotive Works were the three great builders in the last decades of steam. They were hardly the greatest builders in the years after the diesel came into general use, but all three produced the very best in steam, and this was true right until the end of steam production. As the steam locomotive was not a retail product, there were few brand loyalties. True, there were the "special relationships" of the New York Central and Delaware and Hudson with Alco (whose main plant was "on line" to the New York Central at Schenectady, N.Y.) and to a much lesser extent Pennsylvania Railroad's with Baldwin. For the most part, the railroads shopped around for cost advantage and availablility of the product when they wanted it. The railroads seldom manufactured their principal tools, the locomotives and rolling stock needed to do their own work. A conspicuous exception, The Norfolk and Western, "rolled its own" and built many large and powerful locomotives in the great shops at Roanoke, Virginia. But N&W sometimes gave orders to outside builders, and there were N&W items on the Alco book. Pennsylvania had a huge building program at its Juniata shops, but even Pennsy favored Alco with orders—and that relationship lasted into the diesel era. (Make sure that by diesel "diesel-*electric*" is understood. Traction motors ultimately drive the American diesel.)

The big three all survived into the day of general use of the diesel (starting from the late forties), but not with lasting success. Baldwin, after merging with Lima, struggled on a few years and then abandoned the production of diesel machines. Alco had some splendid triumphs, but the late sixties saw its last diesel locomotives built in the United States.

If there was ever a go-getter in the history of American manufacturing, it was the arm of General Motors called Electro-Motive Division (EMD), for it was EMD that not only proved the superiority of the diesel for all types of railway services but that essentially built and marketed this engine to the American railroads. In recent years, only General Electric—a heavily capitalized and skillful builder—has provided American competition to EMD for new locomotives (and *lots* of it at that). EMD's story is comparable to the German domination of the luxury car market in the seventies and eighties; however, even in that case are several vigorous non-German competitors about. Did Alco, Baldwin, and Lima all fail because they lacked the necessary vision? In some ways, the steam builders were ahead, and Alco was extremely prominent in the early development of the diesel switcher. Or was it perhaps that the great steam builders were in the thrall of their traditional customers, and that the top managements and mechanical departments of the big class-one railroads were often dragged, most unwillingly, into the use of the diesel locomotive?

I will dare, in part, to rank the production of Alco in steam. For one thing, Alco produced some of our most beautiful steamers, indeed, perhaps the majority of them. On everybody's list would be its marvelous New York Central Hudson type (see page 77). Among the others: the 4-4-2 of Missouri Pacific from Alco's Brooks Locomotive Works subsidiary, with the characteristic arched or Tudor window that Brooks preferred. There was the Missouri Pacific 6000 (p. 72), which was a perfect end product of the United States Railway Administration designs of World War I, and the Southern Pacific 4-6-0 of 1913, a graceful summing up of locomotive practice of the period before World War I. Also, the Southern Pacific 4-10-2, which, despite its unusual wheel arrangement, was the perfect heavy freight engine of the early twenties (p. 115). Two nominations come from the small Rutland Railroad: its 4-6-2, which was a sort of mini-version of the N.Y.C. Hudson (p. 74) and its 4-8-2 (p. 106). One more entry, a very important one in this Miss America roll call of locomotive beauties: Alco did the prototype series of Nickel Plate 2-8-4's (p. 101), not only aesthetically but also mechanically the true end product of the Super Power era—cleaned up from Lima's famous demonstrator that introduced the 2-8-4 type. The Nickel Plate "Berks"—for some *the* masterpiece of conventional steam—are often attributed to Lima, which did build the later versions, but it was really Alco that got there first with it. As for mechanical achievements in steam, it was really towards the very end of steam—the thirties and forties—that Alco was to have its turn at innovation (and this essay will deal with that shortly).

The great ages of steam locomotive innovation of the last century are chronicled very nicely in these pages. By about 1895 came the first truly high speed passenger engines, 4-4-0's and 4-4-2's with drivers of 78 inches or even taller (pp. 3–39). But railway technology at the turn of the century was still late Victorian—light wooden coaches and short trains. The 1910's saw the coming of the truly big engine—the first machines of the so-called "drag" era, engines of low drivers and large boilers that could move along the hundred of so cars of a "drag" freight at speeds rarely exceeding 35 miles an hour (an ideal speed for hauling bulk commodities such as coal and iron ore). In this period came the 2-10-2 (pp. 112–13) and, even more imposingly, the Mallet compounds, which were two locomotive propulsion machines under a single, very large boiler (pp. 118-29).

In World War I, there was a great standardization and summing up of the steam practice of the period. The locomotives concerned were the graceful and highly influential designs created by the United States Railway Administration—a mysterious activity that has yet to be delineated thoroughly. We know a lot about the careers of such industrial designers as Raymond Loewy and Otto Kuhler, who did famous and spectacular streamlining projects for steam and diesel locomotives and passenger car stock, but virtually nothing about the aesthetically gifted "conventional" designers of USRA. USRA created designs for most standard wheel arrangements then in use for steam. For many observers, this was the golden, or Georgian, period of American steam, when the USRA produced the best-looking designs in the history of our railways. The USRA project might be compared to the comely standardization of American destroyers, cruisers, and auxiliary ships in World War II. For design quality, USRA far exceeded the wartime Liberty and Victory merchant ships. All of the major builders produced the USRA machines,

THE GEORGIAN LOCOMOTIVE. Number 490 of Chesapeake and Ohio's famous F-19 series—power for "The George Washington"—is shown at somewhat later than midpoint in its life-span. The locomotive is shown pretty much as Alco-Richmond outshopped it in 1926, but by 1945 the engine had acquired a large new rectangular "long-distance" tender, which is pictured. Later, in 1950, 490 was radically rebuilt, with streamlined aluminum shroud, four-wheeled truck under an enlarged firebox, and fat, light-weight driving rods equipped with roller bearings. As pictured here, a number of components of 490, including cab and domes, derive from USRA practice.

and USRA designs were employed on virtually all class-one or major railroads. Proof that their engineering was as sound as their good looks is the fact that many locomotives of essentially USRA design were built a decade or so after USRA shut up shop and very few steam engines afterward lacked a detail closely related to some aspect of USRA. USRA engines are found at various places in the book. A good example is C&O 4-8-2 133, on page 105. The very "feel" of the USRA designs and even a literal following of some of the particulars has lasted into the diesel period—in what I call "the USRA style."

There were yet more innovations in steam, in some ways the most important of this century, and they led to what might be called the mature American steam locomotive. With the coming of long express passenger limiteds of all-steel equipment, and of the need for long "hotshots" or time freights on the fastest reasonable schedules, there arose a corresponding need for locomotives of really large horsepower—engines able to keep a heavy load rolling at speeds of 60 to 80 miles per hour. All this led to the Super Power convention—the locomotive that was given a large firebox over a four-wheeled trailing truck set under firebox and cab, a large boiler, and an oversized tender on six-wheeled trucks to minimize the need for frequent refueling. Such engines could manage both heavy trains and fast, tight schedules. It was Lima, the smallest of the three steam builders, that took the lead in this period.

But steam was coming into a critical phase, and towards World War II and for a short period afterwards its proponents would try to build machines that could match

FROM USRA STEAM TO USRA-STYLE DIESEL. Southern 0-8-0 1866, showing the rectangular American Locomotive Company builder's plate (under the stack), was built to USRA plans, with cab, domes, and smokebox front particularly identifiable as USRA designs. The contemporary Long Island road switcher—an EMD Geep—seems to reflect USRA designs in its cab window, shade, trucks, hood over the engines, and treatment of railings and footboards. *(Pictured on right.)*

the growing threat of diesel locomotion. The innovations now were mainly devices to increase fuel efficiency, and they coincided with a few designs that were not only mechanically imposing but flamboyant as well. Alco certainly had its share, perhaps the lion's share, of successful designs in the remarkable last flowering of steam before it began to be shoved aside and then snuffed out completely, owing to the manifold operating and economic advantages of the diesel. A darling of the period and one of the truly unusual engines of the last decade of steam was the streamlined Milwaukee 4-4-2 (p. 38), in which a turn-of-the-century layout was much enlarged and set to work hauling the Milwaukee Road blue-ribbon limited, the Hiawatha,[1] at high speeds. If resurrected today, the Hiawatha 4-4-2 would not at all seem a period piece. It could, with its complimenting train sets, hold its own with the French TGV, the Amtrak Metroliners or any other streamliner of this day. There was also the large and, for its time, ultra-modern New York Central Niagara 4-8-4 (p. 110), all but awash in the efficiency devices of the last days of steam, including poppet valve steam distribution in its cylinders (in the "experimental" 5500 version).

More than anything else, it was the Union Pacific Big Boy of 1941–44 (p. 130) that was Alco's candidate for World's Champion, steam division. Its weight was well over a million pounds, and it could not only pull the equivalent of what used to be called "the whole side of a mountain" but could do this at operating speeds of 70 to 80 miles per hour. By many calculations Big Boy was the largest steam locomotive ever built. It has been called "the epitome of the largest and most efficient steam locomotive on earth."[2]

Is it not curious that the USRA style (or the style of USRA going into Super

---

1. A contemporary Manhattan jazz band, "The Swing Express," uses a view of the Hiawatha 4-4-2 as the logo on its music stands.
2. The quotation is from Jim Kerr, who made a number of useful editorial suggestions for this piece.

Power) has dominated American freight and switcher diesel design from well before the end of steam to the present, and so has dominated the look of such diesels the world over? Look at the cab, the trucks, the hand rails, the footboards, the hood of any of the famous freight diesels of the "hood" or road switcher layout (which is today virtually all contemporary American diesel production), and the ghost of USRA seems to be present. This is especially true of EMD's long and successful series of GP or "Geep" locomotives, Alco's husky-looking Century freight diesels, and General Electric's splendid "U boats," or U series hood units. (Newest GE's are called "dash-8.")

The Alco diesel switcher of 1931 (pp. 143–44) is arguably the prototype of every hood or road switcher since. The early Alco diesel switchers could shunt anywhere in the freight yards of the world today and not look dated or obsolete in the least. I would not be surprised to see one in orange livery handling an Amtrak work train. Perhaps the

CONSEREVATIVE DESIGN IN DIESEL TRACTION MOTOR TRUCKS. The truck pictured is equipment for thousands of American diesels in use today: the Alco AAR four-wheeled truck, which is a somewhat beefed up version of a passenger truck design introduced in the nineteenth century. Its outside mounting of the brake cylinders allows ready application of electric traction motors to both axles.

only thing in transportation as little changed is the Cub-type light monoplane, for the plane young Mathias Rust landed in Red Square, Moscow, hardly differs in looks from the Taylor Cub I modeled in balsa wood in the thirties. This conservatism in light planes and diesel locomotives seems astonishing when you consider the changes in automobiles (Model A Ford to Ford Taurus, say), merchant ships, and commercial and military aircraft over the decades in question. For many, the modern diesel has a very good look—as safe and solid as that of the American federal house.

Many of the surviving Alco diesels ride on a veteran (since the nineteenth century) passenger car truck design, its modernity given away only by the mounting of brake cylinders outside the truck frame and the rounded journal boxes that indicate roller bearings. Other truck designs on contemporary diesels have come from the six-wheeled passenger trucks of 1910 onward or from the one-piece Commonwealth cast-steel trucks used on steam tenders. There are diesel units with the bell mounted over the headlight in best USRA style, and many diesel horns try to approximate the ancient sound of the steam whistle.

There was once a fundamental difference in the planning of steam versus the diesel. Each lot of steam locomotives was a custom design, representing the likes of a given set of mechanical men and top executives, plus a given set of locomotive operating conditions. The diesel was *meant* to be a mass-produced commodity, as automobiles and airplanes are. As this piece will observe, this is not always the case.

The subtle variations in the steam locomotive seem to have been unending. Why does Chesapeake and Ohio 2730 (p. 100) have the sand or large dome ahead of the steam one, as is typical of American practice, though its close cousin, the Nickel Plate 703 (p. 101) reverses the procedure? Look closely at those impeccably handsome USRA-like Mikes or 2-8-2's of L&N and Missouri Pacific on page 97. L&N has a rivet-fabricated trailing truck of the 1910 decade, while Missouri Pacific has the one-piece cast "Delta" trailing truck introduced in the 1920s. The tenders indicate a major difference in fuel used by the locomotives concerned: L&N has the "normal" raised cowl to hold fuel, going two-thirds of the way along the tender indicating it is a coal burner. On Missouri Pacific, the tell-tale fuel tank along the tender top indicates that it burns fuel oil in its firebox. L&N operated in the Appalachian coal fields and Missouri Pacific near the Oklahoma-Texas oil wells, so the difference is logical. Indication of a third cylinder between the outside cylinders is given in the Union Pacific behemoth 9054 (p. 115). This is the existence of a counterweight out-of-synch with the rest. The third cylinder is, by the way, compound expansion (i.e., it uses recycled steam) and the odd driving rod is connected to the oddly counterweighted driving wheel.

Every steam follower likes to observe the type of valve gear on the steamer. The Walscheart valve gear, with its visible rods linking the second or third driver to the top half of the cylinder block, was undoubtedly the most popular. Baker valve gear was more complicated and, some mechanical engineers thought, more efficient. The two types of Baker hangers are perfectly illustrated on page 101. New York Central System 9401, with a horizontal bar scheme, and Nickel Plate Road 7020 with the hanger resembling a mariner's sextant (often used for freight locomotives and almost always for switchers). The earlier locomotives always used the time-honored Stevenson gear, which had a simple link running back to rectangular-topped cylinders (so shaped owing to their so-called slide valve) (see p. 52). It was only in the very last stages of steam that there were persistent attempts at the intricate poppet valve scheme of steam distribution —efficient for fuel but, sadly, maintenance-intensive as well. New York Central 5500 of 1946 (p. 110), mentioned earlier, illustrates one version of the poppet valve scheme.

SUPER REBUILD. The Missouri Pacific 4-4-2, pictured, came from American Locomotive looking as pictured in the plate on page 72. In the immediate post–World War II era, the locomotive, resulting from efforts to match the best mechanical standards of the day, looked as pictured here. Rebuilding has given the engine "disc" driving wheels, cast trailing truck equipped with booster engine (to help starts with heavy trains), new Pyle type headlight, high-speed passenger car trucks under tender, and tender altered to carry fuel oil. The cab now has a sunshade, obscuring the arch of the Tudor window of the original. Some latter-day diesel rebuilds are as extensive as this (though much of the rebuilding may be hidden under the hood enshrouding the diesel motors).

The linking from the driver crosshead to the valves is seemingly so simple as to be incredible. The poppet valve complexities were set *under* the cylinder housing.

A second reason the refinements and variations in steam were barely short of infinite was that the mechanical people at the railways had a penchant for tinkering with designs—both to improve performance and to increase the convenience and safety of the crews. This created an extraordinary *detailed* diversity in the appearance of American steam—given that the general appearance of American steam from the rest of the world's was almost immediately recognizable. Obviously, for many enthusiasts, that has provided an unending pastime. (I will say more about diesel rebuilding at the end of this essay.) Rebuilds were rarely as radical as that for Missouri Pacific 1198 (see illustration), in which a 1910 engine is given the technology of the late forties, with roller bearings, "disk" drivers, a cast trailer truck under the cab, a new bell arrangement, and a tender altered to carry oil. Compare it to its original design (p. 39). Hard not to conclude the original engine has it all over the rebuilt version as far as good looks go, but fans often feel rebuildings radically improved the looks of some engines. The rebuilding of Missouri Pacific 1198 seems roughly comparable to what would be the effect of equipping a pre–World War I Packard with all the options available for a late-model BMW.

As for differences in supposedly standardized production models of the diesel, they can show up conspicuously even in builder's photos, even before the locomotive shops and rebuilders have added *their* modifications to the standard models. For diversity in the units as they come from the builders, consider page 157. All pictures are of RS3 road switcher units but each cab is slightly different: Reading's with its brief rain gutter over the cab window, Pennsylvania's with its cab shade very much in the style of American steam. There are even two types of horn mounting shown on the four engines. Reading carries a smaller fuel tank (under the running boards). Pennsylvania has the road's characteristic road phone antennae along the top of its hood. New York Central and Pennsylvania have a different style of stack than Reading and Piedmont and Northern.

The best reference books on diesel identification, by the way, are the Jerry A. Pinkepank and Louis A. Marre *Diesel Spotter's Guide* publications (Kalmbach Publishing Company, Milwaukee).

There remains to speak of Alco's electrics, for the firm was a major "player" in that field before the thirties. Conspicuous were the "steeple cab" electrics of the New York Central (p. 137), which inspired the most famous toy locomotives of the first decades of the century—from Lionel and other makers. Conspicuous also were such oddities as the many-windowed electrics for Virginian, and Norfolk and Western, with side rods attached to large spoked wheels. These looked for all the world like facades of a village street being carried above the rodding of a steam locomotive (p. 138).

Alco survives for me at Speonk, N.Y., a terminal point on the Long Island Railroad for a good number of trains on the Montauk Branch. The longer trains on the Montauk line still (at this writing) have an Alco FA2 streamliner ca. 1952 on the West, or New York, end—rarities that must send numbers of fans on tours across several states to see and photograph them. But the FA2's are now virtually only car bodies with cab controls

STREAMLINED ALCO SURVIVOR. The FA2 unit is standard equipment on the West, or New York, end of Long Island Railroad trains on the Montauk branch and the trains from Huntington to Port Jefferson. The locomotive is outwardly little changed from the day it came from the builder's yards at Schenectady, N.Y., in 1952, but its power is used only to work train heating or air conditioning. The longevity in 609 approaches that for many of the steamers that lasted into the 1940s, in a day when streamlined diesels have become a rarity on United States rails. The standard locomotive on the East, or Atlantic Ocean, end of the same Long Island trains is the GP40 road switcher pictured on page xi.

and powered only to supply air conditioners and train heat.[3] Alco will continue to survive, if only as the original maker of components used in rebuilds.[4] Smart railway money now often prefers to rebuild older machines—exactly as in steam days—and the rebuilders are giving the builders of new locomotives tremendous competition. The strange contemporary trade of modification or rebuilding is leading to a great diversity in the mechanical details and even the appearance of modern diesels. In the rebuilds, one maker's cab and hood may be married to another's diesel motors and trucks. or it may be to some permutation of this. There may be various cowls, blisters, louvres, grills, stacks added to take care of such "options" as dynamic braking, turbochargers, after coolers, and steam generators (the last to create steam heat for engines that handle passenger cars). All of this is, of course, a continuing source of delight to the serious enthusiast.

H. Stafford Bryant, Jr.
December 1989

3. I am indebted for this information to Charles B. Castner of the Family Lines System (Louisville and Nashville), who read the essay and made a number of suggestions for improving it.
4. The Introduction to this book (see page 1) has a good account of the sale of the Alco locomotive manufacture in Schenectady in 1969 to a Canadian firm now called Bombardier, Inc.

ACKNOWLEDGMENTS

The Trustees, Manager, and Staff of Alco Historic Photos

Except as noted, the photographs, mechanical drawings and other illustrations in this book are reproductions from original negatives, engineering records and other archival material owned by the City of Schenectady, Alco Products, Inc., and/or the American Locomotive Company Historical Society. These collections are among the archival holdings maintained and administered by Alco Historic Photos, an organization incorporated under the Education Law of the State of New York. Readers interested in further information on these collections are invited to write to: Alco Historic Photos, Post Office Box 21, Albany, NY 12201-0021.

INTRODUCTION

The American Locomotive Company, commonly known as Alco, together with its predecessor locomotive companies, has experienced a long and glorious locomotive building history, producing in excess of 90,000 locomotives in steam, diesel-electric, and electric, easily qualifying for the title of the greatest locomotive builder. A predecessor company, Rogers of Paterson, New Jersey, in 1837 had the honor of building Sandusky, America's first steam locomotive, while another predecessor, Schenectady of Schenectady, New York, in 1847 built Lightning, its first locomotive, which quickly established a world speed record of 60 mph. Most predecessor locomotive companies of Alco came under its control early in this century. Soon all of its domestic locomotive production was concentrated in the huge Schenectady complex while it was also operating Montreal Locomotive Works (MLW), a subsidiary in Montreal, Quebec. When locomotive building ceased at Schenectady in 1969, Alco continued production of their famous 251 Series diesel engines at their Auburn, New York, plant. Manufacturing rights to the Century Series locomotive were sold to the Montreal operation, today owned by Bombardier, Inc., who manufacture the M-Line locomotives for Canadian domestic use, and the MX-Line for their international market, with licensing rights to build the 251 Series diesel engines in their Montreal plant for their own locomotives. Illustrations of Montreal-built diesel-electric locomotives both current and past are included on pages 195–219. Alco locomotives have had the distinction of hauling many of the world's most famous passenger trains and high-speed freight trains across the globe.

This book contains a condensed history of Alco followed by a chronology of notable Alco achievements and a treasury of quality builder's photographs representative of locomotive production over the years with accompanying captions. Experts agree that builder's photographs are the ultimate, as they invariably were photographed professionally and accurately reflect the locomotive as it appeared brand new. All locomotives illustrated in this book are of Standard Gauge (4'-8½" or 1435 mm between the rails), except where otherwise noted in the captions. The book has been divided into three main groups: Steam locomotives have been subdivided by wheel arrangement for comparison, from the smallest tank engine to the greatest articulateds. Within each wheel arrangement locomotives are listed alphabetically by railway, road number, wheel arrangement, date built, driving wheel diameter in inches, and weight in tons of the locomotive and tender, respectively. Electric locomotives have the same caption data, with the addition of horsepower rating. A special section of diesel-electric locomotives follows the section on electric locomotives and also includes the builder model.

Illustrated Treasury

of the

American Locomotive Company

William H. Vanderbilt   600   4-4-0   1880

Canada Central   5   4-4-0   1879

Union Pacific   675 4-4-0

Denver, South Park & Pacific   Gauge 3'-0"   63 2-8-0   1883

Metropolitan Elevated RR-NYC   48   2-4-2T 1879

Illinois Central   232   2-6-4T 1892

Ulster & Delaware   1   4-6-0   1892

New York Central   1550 2-D-2   1928   750HP

Carolina & Northwestern   11 RS11   1955   1800HP

Duluth, Winnipeg & Pacific   3601 RS11   1956   1800HP

Duluth, Missabe & Iron Range   55 RSD15 1959 2400HP

Southern Pacific   7005 RSD12 1960 1800HP

Erie Mining Co.   300 C420   1955   2000HP

Long Island RR   205 C420   1963   2000HP

Erie — Lackawanna   2454 C425   1964   2500HP

Reading Lines   5212 C430   1966   3000HP

THE BEGINNINGS
ALCO AT SCHENECTADY, N.Y.

ALCO's interest in progressive transportation began near the end of the War of 1812, with George W. Featherstonhaugh. Ten years before 1825, he began educating the public to the advantages of building railroads, but in 1825 he put his dream into action by applying for a charter, which was granted on April 17, 1826.

Construction began in 1830, and the Mohawk and Hudson Railroad opened formally a year later. On August 13, 1831, the Dewitt Clinton drew its first passenger train to Schenectady, N.Y., bringing a young and vital new industry to the Mohawk Valley, which became the New York State center of railroad construction.

Other lines sprang up. 1832 saw the Saratoga and Schenectady Railroad, later to become part of the Delaware and Hudson. The year 1843 brought the Troy and Schenectady Railroad. True, the travel time was, by our standards, tedious—the 160-mile journey from Albany, N.Y. to Auburn, N.Y. took 13 hours,—but no matter. The events of the early 1800's ushered in a new and romantic chapter of American history—the age of the railroad.

GROWING PAINS

In 1847, Platt Potter and John Ellis joined other free-thinking citizens of Schenectady to see about establishing a manufacturing works to construct locomotives. To aid in the worthy project, Potter and Ellis invited the three Norris brothers of Philadelphia, whose booming reputation as locomotive craftsmen had rapidly reached New York ears.

Ellis and Potter were confident of raising $30,000, but a December 6, 1847 letter from the Norrises brought sad tidings:

". . . The necessary capital required will be $50,000 dollars to purchase the ground, erect buildings and necessary tools and machinery . . We certainly could with this amount ($30,000) commence, but not with any advantage to the present propriety of the works . . ."

As a result, Potter and Ellis called a fund-raising meeting. There was doubt in the community; as one prominent citizen put it, "Once the railroads entering Schenectady are supplied with locomotives, what will you do with your locomotives after you have built them?"

Nonetheless, most of the money was raised by subscription, with the Norris brothers demonstrating their faith in the project by contributing $10,576 in tools and machinery. In 1848, The Schenectady Locomotive Engine Manufactory was founded and, within a year, produced a fittingly celebrated locomotive: the "Lightning."

THE "LIGHTNING"

Most of Schenectady's 6,000 citizens lined the streets to witness the debut of an engine destined to revolutionize railway locomotion. Weighing 15 tons, possessing 84" drivers, the "Lightning" was designed for unprecedented high speeds. It was rated to pull nine cars at nine to fifteen miles an hour, but once pulled an eight-car train at eighty miles per hour!

This historic locomotive, unfortunately, was far too advanced for its time. So great was its drive that it actually caused damage to the roadbed and had to be retired. Its exciting career cut short, the "Lightning" was, most likely, reduced to scrap to aid the Civil War effort.

DARK DAYS AND NEW LIFE

The "Lightning's" untimely demise presaged a bleak era for the works. Orders failed to materialize; even worse, the discouraged Norrises abandoned the project. But John Ellis was undeterred, and in 1851, he took charge of the newly-formed Schenectady Locomotive Works.

Ellis's faith served him well. The Canandaigua and Corning Railroad Company trusted him with the building of a new and interesting "Great Western" locomotive. Within six months of receiving the order, the Schenectady Locomotive Works turned out this unusual engine.

Perhaps Ellis's greatest talent was his ability to

select exceptional personnel. In 1852, he appointed, as Master Mechanic, one Walter McQueen, who gained so great a reputation as a designer of locomotives that Schenectady locomotives were known for years as "McQueen Engines."

Under this combination of new leadership and outstanding talent, the Company flourished for several years, until a general business panic, in 1857, crippled not only the Nation's economy, but that of the Schenectady Locomotive Works. As the Company's confidence slumped, Ellis's associates, hoping to force his hand, asked him to name a price at which he would sell his stock. They agreed to do the same, but were astonished when Ellis, having arranged a bank loan that would enable him to do so, accepted their outrageously, inflated selling price, and bought them out instead.

THE CIVIL WAR

With the advent of the War between the States, John Ellis took a tremendous risk. Without an order on the books, he ordered construction of a great many locomotives. His gamble paid off, for between 1861 and 1863, the Government purchased every one of the Works' 84 locomotives. The plant bustled with activity during this period, and from the war-inspired fervor, many a sentimental story sprang up around the locomotives.

For example, in 1862, a Schenectady Locomotive Works' engine stopped near the Virginia camp of Schenectady's 134th Regiment. The homesick boys swarmed about the familiar locomotive, tearfully patting it as if it were a favorite horse.

BACK ON THE TRACKS

The prosperity, sparked by the Civil War, continued well past Appomattox. Indeed, there were disastrous setbacks—in 1866, a blaze consumed most of the Works' main building, while in 1869, the Mohawk River overflowed, inundating the plant—but the plant's dedication to progress prevailed.

About this time, the works completed the historic "Jupiter # 60." A wood-burning locomotive, it was shipped around Cape Horn to Sacramento, California. Its first assignment was to transport ex-governor Leland Stanford and his party from Sacramento to Promontory Point, Utah, where the rails of the Central Pacific and Union Pacific Railroads met on May 10, 1869; thus, the Jupiter became the first locomotive to pass over the rails of these two historic roads.

Expanded activity was the rule of the few years ahead. In 1876, a sleek, new locomotive, named simply "Number 266" was completed. Its performance was to startle railroad experts the world over. It made a run of 81 miles in 82 minutes—the fastest sustained operation recorded up to that time.

During the 1880's, a prominent railroad figure came on the scene. Albert J. Pitkin, renowned for his work at the Baldwin Locomotive and Rhode Island Locomotive Works, was a far-sighted advocate of large boilers and increased grate areas. His design for the cross-compound engine, which economized on both coal and water through an ingenious cylinder system, marked him as a pioneer in conservationist technology.

By 1900, production output hit a high of 417 locomotives for the year. The engines were so advanced that the average weight of a locomotive was well over 60 tons—better than 4 times the weight of the original "Lightning!" The increase of foreign orders necessitated the rapid expansion of the Schenectady Locomotive Works, and Pitkin's heavy American-style locomotives garnered fame throughout the world.

ALCO AND THE AUTOMOBILE

Though ALCO announced its decision to enter the automotive business in 1905, it had been commissioned in 1904 by a French Company, Automobile M. Berliet, to manufacture the Berliet automobile.

Albert Pitkin, who guided ALCO's auto manufacturing, immediately announced the construction of a new plant for automobile production in Providence, Rhode Island. The New York Times hailed the Berliet venture as "the first instance of an American concern making a foreign car with American material and by American labor, complete in every detail."

Initially, the Company was determined to use only European parts and materials until it was satisfied that "equally as good or better can be obtained in the United States." Eventually, however, as the state of the American art progressed, this policy changed to the point where even the Berliet license was dropped in 1908. The automobile now proudly proclaimed the ALCO name.

The "ALCO" was a superior car, presented at private exhibitions and attracting attention wherever it went. Its success occasioned its company to spend a half-million in expanding its auto facilities. A solid, durable machine, it was "built like a locomotive;" its promoters were quick to stress its "mystic element vanadium, the anti-fatigue metal." "It stays new," was the promo slogan of the day.

RACY DAYS

One man's pride and faith in the ALCO car transcended anyone's. Henry Fortune Grant, the chief test driver for ALCO in 1906, hankered to race the cars he tested. Providence plant officials were inflexibly opposed, but in 1907, when Grant left to work for C. F. Whitney, a Boston ALCO dealer, he got a go-ahead signal. Whitney bought a 40 HP ALCO car from the factory, and Henry Fortune Grant's own fortune quickly turned in his favor.

Grant impressed ALCO and was soon racing for the Company team. He drove a 6-cylinder ALCO car to victory in 1909's Vanderbilt Cup Race, averaging a then-astounding 62.81 MPH. In the even more spectacular 1910 contest, 300,000 spectators watched Henry and his "Bete Noire," ('black beast,' as the car was nicknamed) shatter records, winning with an average speed of 65.18 MPH. ALCO and Grant retired from racing in 1911, but not before they had provided the Vanderbilt Cup Race with its fastest race ever.

A SPECTACULAR FINISH

To all appearances, ALCO's automotive line continued to thrive. Their showing at the Vanderbilt Cup Race, their reputation for unexcelled quality, craftsmanship, and elegance, their versatility—all bespoke an auto that would lead its field for years.

Imagine the shock, then, when an August 22, 1913 New York Times headline blared, "ALCO Makers Quit Automobile Field."

Automobile Row was stunned, especially when, two days later, American Locomotive revealed its overall gross earning for the fiscal year—$34,000,000, the largest in Company history. Yet President W. H. Marshall tersely informed stockholders that automobile production was discontinued because "it was unprofitable."

The demise of the ALCO auto can be attributed to poor communication and management. The Company had invested between 4 and 6 million dollars in the auto, yet only 5,000 units had, in fact, been manufactured in the Company's seven years in the field. ALCO, in actuality, lost an average of $460.00 on each vehicle built. Also, a tragic lack of communication between Sales and Purchasing was a major contributor to the downfall; for example, in 1912, Sales advised ordering materials for 800 trucks. Purchasing bought materials for 1600. Truck sales that year: 750.

Despite the flurry of accusations, rumors, and innuendos that surrounded the end of ALCO's auto years, however, one charge was never made: no one ever said that the ALCO was not a great car.

CASEY JONES

Of all American folk heroes, none has a more enduring place in the hearts of railway folk than ALCO's own Casey Jones. The brave engineer and Ol' 382 rode to immortal glory on April 30, 1900. Travelling at 70 mph, the Cannonball Special plowed into a freight train that had no business being where it was. The fireman jumped to safety, but Casey stayed at the controls, trying valiantly to brake to a stop.

The Ol' 382 was made of tough stuff; though Casey died instantly, it only took a little over a thousand dollars in repairs to keep the Cannonball Special rolling for another 35 years—despite its having crashed through a caboose, a car loaded with corn, another filled with hay, and yet another full of lumber!

Ol' 382 was scrapped in 1935, unfortunately, but she and her brave engineer live on in ballad after ballad. Casey's tombstone bears the inspiring legend: "For I'm going to run till she leaves the rail/or make it on time with the southbound mail."

BACK TO LOCOMOTIVES

Through all this, the ALCO locomotive continued to thrive and expand. In 1917, the first issue of Forbes proclaimed ALCO number 61 on a list of America's top 100 businesses. ALCO streamlined in the 1920's, closing down its smallest plants and bringing the bulk of its talent back to Schenectady, and in 1926, it embarked on yet another progressive phase: the diesel-electric locomotives.

As early as 1904, ALCO had experimented with electric locomotives, but in 1924, it produced the first succesful diesel-electric for the Central Railroad of New Jersey. Its interest whetted, ALCO agreed to build experimental locomotives for New York Central. One was to be used for suburban passenger service, the other for local freight duty. The passenger unit broke records for cylinder specifications, but failed so frequently that it was soon withdrawn from service. Luckily, the freight unit fared better.

While the freight unit was too small to be termed an unqualified success, it proved that a diesel engine could indeed make a go of it beyond yard limits. Hence, it earned a small, but significant, niche in rail history. Despite the mixed results of these experiments, ALCO thought enough of the diesel's future to purchase the McIntosh & Seymour Company of

Auburn, New York.

THE BEGINNING ALCO AT AUBURN N.Y.

About sixty years after Ellis realized his dream of a locomotive company, John E. McIntosh and James A. Seymour had a dream of their own, taking shape in a former tack factory in the swamps on the west side of Auburn, New York. What Ellis had seen in the railroads, they saw in steam engines; over the next thirty years, their small factory grew from a little known local venture to a world-famous industry.

McIntosh & Seymour emphasized three things: power, quality, and innovation. Their first steam-engine was as good an example of this as their last; sold to a sawmill in Moravia, N. Y. for $725.00, it gave almost constant everyday service until the mill was destroyed in a fire. Then the engine, salvaged later from the ruins, was overhauled and put to use in the George S. Cady & Son factory; McIntosh & Seymour, out of sentiment, offered to purchase the engine back when it no longer served its purpose. That was in 1925.

Cady answered wryly: ". . . we will be glad to do as you wish. However, as this engine has been out 39 years and is still working as nicely as when first put into operation, it is difficult to estimate or guess as to what year, or even century, the change in ownership can be made to take place."

The first engine was a hardy, single-cylinder engine; as the company grew, so did its products. McIntosh & Seymour made some of the world's largest horizontal and vertical steam engines. The Company won awards at the 1901 Pan-American Exposition for the quality of its product and for its advanced, innovative engineering features.

There are, however, limits to innovation; the best of products becomes outmoded. The steam turbine replaced the steam engine; by 1911, McIntosh & Seymour faced a $100,000 loss in sales. Improvement of the steam-engine was no longer the best source.

A better course became available in 1912; the patent rights of Dr. Rudolph Diesel expired, and American manufacturers began, in conjunction with their European counterparts, developing diesel engines. James Seymour, consulted with Dr. Diesel himself, then with a Swedish manufacturer. The Swedish design, with certain features demanded by American engine practice, was adopted by McIntosh & Seymour, and the Auburn plant swung into the new venture.

As with the steam-engines, McIntosh & Seymour attempted to produce long-lasting, economical engines for innovative uses. The first known installation of A. C. generators driven in parallel by diesel engines was supplied with McIntosh & Seymour engines. This was in 1915; the same engines were moved to power a broadcasting station in 1939.

During World War I, the diesel engines supplied by McIntosh & Seymour saved costs and lives: the same engine that had made the submarine possible enabled ships to evade undersea attack. All diesel engines emitted an exhaust which was, in comparison to the tell-tale smoke-plume of the steam-vessels, nearly invisible; diesel ships avoided sighting and attack much more rapidly than steamships. In addition, McIntosh & Seymour worked rapidly to develop a marine diesel engine that could reverse directions rapidly, thereby increasing the ships' maneuverability. Their design quickly dominated their engine production, so that they could provide engines for the ships being constructed for the United States Government.

By now, McIntosh & Seymour held several distinctions. It now produced the largest 4-stroke diesel engines in America, it had produced the largest and most popular reciprocating prime movers for steam power in America, and it was the world's largest plant exclusively devoted to building diesel engines. Perhaps the highest praise of their product, however, came in an odd form. During a hurricane in Florida, an ALCO service engineer on a courtesy call to a municipal light plant, removed a crankcase door on a diesel generator and crawled inside it with rags, spare coveralls, an electric droplight, and a copy of The Saturday Evening Post. The roof of the light-plant had begun to come off,

and the diesel engine seemed to him the safest place in Florida to spend the night. The innovative use of diesel-engines was, after all, a company trademark.

THE ALCO DIESEL-ELECTRIC LOCOMOTIVE

In 1927, McIntosh & Seymour introduced their first diesel engine for a purpose that, today, it is hard to think of ever having been innovative: a locomotive engine. Other companies were involved in the final product: A. C. F. Brill Co. made the cab, and General Electric Company (U.S.A.) the electrical equipment. The locomotive was sold to the Lehigh Valley Railroad; before the year was out, the New York Central Railroad purchased an 8-cylinder engine of the same type for use in a passenger car. In 1929, the New York Central Railroad purchased a 12-cylinder motor from McIntosh & Seymour for use in a passenger locomotive. The cab and chassis for that locomotive were built by the American Locomotive Company of Schenectady.

ALCO immediately recognizing the future of these engines in railroading, negotiated an option to purchase McIntosh & Seymour. The stock-market crash left ALCO in much the same risky position Ellis had found himself in after the Panic of 1857. Like Ellis, however, the present company decided to take the risk, and bought McIntosh & Seymour in December 1929. Despite the severity of the depression that followed, the move proved a wise one; due, among other factors, to the need for replacement parts on Dust-Bowl damaged engines in the Midwest, McIntosh & Seymour had work and income for employees and for itself. In 1933, a bleak year for many businesses, McIntosh & Seymour earned the greatest income of any division of ALCO.

ALCO SCHENECTADY & AUBURN

Between 1930 and 1936, ALCO's product altered considerably, as did demand. Diesel switchers were replacing steam; by 1935, ALCO was producing 20 % more diesel locomotives than it was steam engines. As Henry Ford brought standardized parts and mass production to the auto industry, the locomotive industry scrambled to do the same. ALCO, in the the process, produced an engine so successful in its "cold start" test that all rights to the product were snapped up by a surprising bidder: The United States Navy. The steel industry had been experimenting with (then new) "exotic" alloys; ALCO constructed two experimental engines from the lighter, stronger alloys, and, through the knowledge gained, laid the foundation for the entire future diesel engine program.

Not all experiments were successful. Returning to Europe for ideas, ALCO entered an agreement with the Sulzer brothers of Switzerland, allowing ALCO to make two types of the Sulzer engines. The engines proved to be too heavy, producing fewer horsepower per pound than other engines then under development. Still, at the same time, ALCO was experimenting with the 2-cycle Sulzer engines, it was developing a more efficient 4-cycle engine; if one line of research proved a failure, others did not.

Even the steam locomotives, though declining in popularity, were improved upon during these years; ALCO introduced the "Hiawatha." Built for the Chicago, Milwaukee, and St. Paul Railroad, it had a top speed of over 120 MPH and a capability of continued operation at 100 MPH.

1936 saw the Golden Jubilee of McIntosh & Seymour, which shortly became known as the Diesel Engine Division, American Locomotive Company. During the next five years, bigger was better for the designers at ALCO—with the exception of such sidelines as watertight doors and windows, controllable from the bridge, for the liner "America" and other passenger ships, ALCO concentrated on increasing power and size in locomotives.

In 1936, ALCO installed its first exhaust driven turbocharger on its own 6-cylinder engine, thereby increasing it from 600 to 900 HP. Dr. Buchi himself, inventor of the turbocharger, supervised the application; ALCO was licensed as one of his initial U.S. outlets.

In 1939, ALCO delivered its first 2000 HP streamlined passenger locomotive to the Chicago, Rock Island & Pacific Railroad; difficulties in synchronizing the two engines which powered it were corrected in the "200" series which followed it.

In 1941, ALCO built the largest locomotive in the world. Named "Big Boy" and bought by the Union Pacific Railroad, the mammoth mallet locomotive had sixteen 68" drive wheels, achieved 7,000 HP, and could haul a mile-long freight train at a mile a minute.

In the final years of this period, however, ALCO developed new concerns. Uneasy over the war in Europe, the United States began building for defence; ALCO's Auburn plant built a substantial number of engines for the Navy. At the same time, ALCO undertook the development of an alternative to the old engines, whose cast-iron components shattered readily in combat. Unfortunately, development of this alternative engine was delayed by more immediate wartime needs just as the engine models were ready for testing; the Government directed ALCO to limit its diesel engine activities to providing power for switching locomotives, submarines, sub-chasers, and minesweepers.

The engines were tested in 1944-45; at roughly the same time ALCO's Board of Directors announced that diesel locomotives would replace steam in the postwar years. A group of engineers from Fairbanks Morse was hired. Schenectady's Diesel Engineering Department was reorganized, and new products came out in 1945 and 1946, combining almost all that had been learned in the previous years: a 4-cycle, 12-cylinder, V-type 1500 HP engine for freight service and a similar 16-cylinder, 2000 HP engine for passenger service. By the late 1940's about 65 % of all diesel-electric switching locomotives in service on U.S. railroads were built by ALCO.

ALCO AND WORLD WAR II

Innovation on diesel engines for civilian use may have halted at ALCO during the war, but ALCO was not idle, merely too busy in other fields. As Ellis's company had built locomotives for the Civil War, and McIntosh and Seymour's company had supplied marine engines in World War I while ALCO had built still more locomotives, so in World War II, ALCO produced, re-tooled, and responded to American combat needs.

The needs were many and varied—usually massive as well. ALCO, with no experience in the field, was the first company in America to produce M-3 "General Grant" tanks, 6,000 of them before the company was called on for a more urgent need. The War Department, it seemed, needed motive power, and badly. That, at least, ALCO had done before, and did it again; during World War II, ALCO produced 1,036 steam and 157 diesel-electric locomotives for the War Department.

America's needs changed again. ALCO was directed to build M-36 tanks—"Sluggers," the tank men called them—to fight the Nazi's Tiger Tanks in France. The order was urgent, time short. The last of ALCO's "Sluggers" was delivered in December 1944—the month of the Battle of the Bulge; ALCO had provided a new sort of cavalry to come over the hill in time.

ALCO fought against tanks, as well as providing them. At El Alamein, Rommel, the 'Desert Fox,' was himself outfoxed when a secret weapon appeared: The M-7, a 105mm cannon, mounted on a mobile carrier made in Schenectady and run through the streets to the testing grounds and the shipping depot without any information regarding it having leaked out. ALCO built a total of 3,314 M-7's, 1000 of them coming into play at El Alamein.

If innovation at ALCO was great, production was magnificent. Diesel engines for minesweepers, patrol boats, repair ships, mine layers, and Navy tug boats poured out of Auburn; in addition, the Army used some Auburn-built engines to replace bombed-out power stations in occupied countries.

ALCO's most satisfying part in the war effort was in what it understood best—railroading. A Collier's magazine article, "Casey Jones Goes to War," (May 20, 1944) by Amy Porter, tells the story:

In late 1942, with the Mediterranean closed to Allied shipping and the Murmansk convoy route blocked by enemy submarines, Russia called urgently for more supplies. Supplies landed en masse at Persian Gulf ports barely trickled into Russia. The inadequately powered Trans-Iranian Railway was the bottleneck.

In barely 650 miles of track, this railway afforded nearly every obstacle engineers could face. 150 miles of desert, 7,000-foot mountains, a temperature range from 170°F in the desert to −40° in the mountains, 225 tunnels and literally thousands of bridges. British and American steam locomotives were not powerful enough to haul much freight under these conditions; it took most of their power to haul their own coal and water through the rugged trip. More powerful locomotives were needed, badly and quickly.

ALCO representatives were called to Washington, and asked if they could get some diesel electrics to Iran quickly—meanwhile converting the axle arrangement somehow so that the Iranian road could bear the 120-ton weight. ALCO could and did; by the first week of December that same year, 29 1000-HP diesels with six axles, instead of the standard four, landed at the Persian Gulf—along with a newly-recruited 800-man American Locomotive Shop battalion, dedicated to keeping those 29 diesels rolling.

Joel Sayre's book, Persian Gulf Command (Random House), takes up the story from here. It was no easy story; the squabble between steam and diesel proponents, carried over from the states, continued under the worst of conditions in Iran. Finally, even the steam diehards admitted that the diesels saved the railroaders lives in the tunnels: "There were 47 miles of tunnels, all unventilated, and when the long ones were filled with smoke and steam from the steam locomotives, the temperature rose to 180°. Then one day the diesels arrived and took over in the tunnels, and the torture ended." So did the threat to Russian supply-lines; the Russian's needs were exceeded by 18%.

ALCO served not only America's needs, but those of its allies. 150 Scotch marine boilers were ordered for the British Supply Mission and the U.S. Navy. Using mass-production methods on the first order of 90, ALCO had completed three of them five days ahead of contract time, and completed the last unit 9 months ahead of schedule. ALCO also made marine engine forgings for British ocean-going vessels, and even did a few forgings for an ally closer to home, a business associate from before the war: General Electric (U.S.A.). (ALCO's business in forgings included those for Navy torpedoes, produced from the Schenectady plant, and large caliber gun barrels for the War Department.)

At the war's end, General Douglas MacArthur stood on the foredeck of the battleship "Missouri" as the Japanese signed their surrender terms. Above him were other witnesses: the mammoth 16" guns, mounted on turret rollers made in ALCO's Schenectady plant and precision-machined for United States battleships.

ALCO, and its employees, surely deserved that representation. During the war, ALCO workers had produced more than a billion dollars worth of war materials; the Company itself risked millions of dollars of its own capital, often without waiting for contract formalities. With a war time profit of only 2.5%, the Company produced some of the lowest-cost munitions of the war effort.

ALCO
1945-1950

On September 14, 1945, ALCO announced that it had purchased the Beaumont Iron Works Company of Beaumont, Texas. The war was over, and ALCO was back in business for itself. ALCO took over management of the Beaumont plant that October, thereby entering the field of oil well drilling-and-production equipment. This was not merely expansion, but foresight: ALCO, at the time, was among the world's foremost manufacturers of heat exchanger equipment, and had many of those units located in the Beaumont area. With the purchase of the Beaumont plant, the Company could offer better service for the heat exchanger equipment located there.

The following year, ALCO's sales totaled $115,074,123, most of this coming from the manufacture of steam locomotives. Despite ALCO's announcement of a few years before, in 1946, the conflict between steam and diesel locomotives was far from over; 75% of all locomotive production consisted of steam locomotives, principally for shipment abroad. Many Eurasian nations, their own plants in ruins, were clamoring for locomotives to replace those destroyed by the war. They turned to America, and to ALCO, for those locomotives.

ALCO's own efficiency as a wartime supplier and an ordnance manufacturer put it at a business disadvantage at home. While other companies went back to producing diesel locomotives, ALCO was asked to continue ordnance production. Thereafter, the Company faced the the problems of changing from steam to diesel locomotive production and making up for lost diesel locomotive sales. In 1947, ALCO initiated an all-out campaign for its diesel-electric locomotives.

This was a changeover as revolutionary as it was involved, both mechanically and economically. Steam locomotives were built to order, custom or contract engineering jobs; if a locomotive was built, it had a buyer. Diesel-electrics were manufactured as standardized, assembly-line products. In diesel locomotive production, great amounts of money could be—at times, were—tied up in inventory.

ALCO already had an impressive line of standardized diesel locomotives, both freight and passenger. In 1947, ALCO introduced a new diesel-electric locomotive, a 16-cylinder, 2000 HP model. ALCO was back in the diesel locomotive business, making up for lost time.

In 1948, ALCO celebrated 100 years of locomotive building in Schenectady. On that year, a steam locomotive, a 2-8-4 with 63" drivers, was built for the Pittsburgh and Lake Erie Railroad. It left the plant on June 18, the last steam locomotive to be built by ALCO. With regret from some veterans, and excitement from many, ALCO had successfully made a complete conversion from steam to diesel-electric locomotives.

Conversions of this kind were not small-scale for ALCO; the Company had six plants—the Schenectady and Auburn plants; plus one in Dunkirk, New York; the recently-purchased plant in Beaumont; a plant in Latrobe, Pennsylvania; and one in Chicago Heights, Illinois. Other changes and expansions came rapidly. ALCO received the first contract from the Atomic Energy Commission (AEC) to produce a nickel-plated pipe at its Dunkirk plant and its newly-acquired Cincinnati, Ohio plant.

ALCO-DUNKIRK

ALCO's plant at Dunkirk had such a widely varied line of products and activities that it is worth considering apart from the rest of ALCO. When the Schenectady Locomotive Works merged with seven locomotive building companies in 1901 to form ALCO, the Brooks Locomotive Works in Dunkirk, which had produced steam locomotives since 1869, was one of those companies.

The Dunkirk plant, after having produced roughly 4200 units, sold its last steam locomotive in 1931 and went into manufacturing thermal products, including pressure vessels, pipe, heat exchangers, and many other related products. As the line grew and changed, this facility was renamed "ALCO Thermal Products Division;" it was a central feature of ALCO's new projected image and capability of diversification.

Dunkirk's chief product was adaptability to any technical demand; both its plant and its personnel were suited for a wide range of requests. The facility covered approximately 50 acres and employed as many as 2200 people. Machinery included a 750-ton hydraulic press, a 1500-ton crimper, a massive hydraulic ram, a 25' boring mill, intricate machinery to wrap coppersmith around tubing, and a monstrous roll that could bend steel anywhere from 1/8" to 4" thick. Production included multi-purpose air-coolers that could serve for diesel engines, steam condensing where high vacuums were not needed, and vapor or gas cooling and condensing. (These exchangers were also made in the Beaumont plant, which operated an exchanger repair center servicing the entire

Southwest.) Sixty percent of all the exchangers used to process aviation gasoline during World War II were made by ALCO or to ALCO designs. ALCO-Dunkirk also produced 40% of all the exchangers used for making synthetic rubber in World War II.

ALCO-Dunkirk also made water preparation units which could make salt water fresh, exhaust gas coolers for use in wind tunnels, oil refining pressure vessels called fractionating towers or reactors, portable field boilers used by oil men for drilling in out-of-the-way places, and a cement kiln weighing over a million pounds. In addition, Dunkirk made pipe of every shape, size and requirement.

Dunkirk's expertise, in both piping and pressure vessels, combined in unlikely places. Dunkirk provided the shield used as a work chamber for the sandhogs who dug New York City's Lincoln Tunnel. The same ALCO technology went into the construction of the Brooklyn Battery Tunnel and others. Over 100 Dunkirk-built air coolers were in use in Trans-Arabian pipeline stations. The International Airport, at Idlewild, was served by a 10-mile network of ALCO water pipe. (Dunkirk was assisted in its pipe manufacturing enterprises by ALCO's other pipe making facility in Cincinnati, Ohio.) The huge steel towers supporting the roadway of the Tri-Borough Bridge were built at Dunkirk. On a typical work day, Dunkirk would ship 35 carloads of products.

ALCO AND THE ATOM

The Atomic Age had arrived, and with it the need for thousands of new manufacturing operations to supply enormous quantities of newly-conceived equipment. As the equipment was put into manufacture, it became almost immediately apparent that, as with any new product, improvements were necessary. ALCO was heavily involved in both production and improvement.

The nickel-plated steel pipe, requested by the Atomic Energy Commission, is a good example of the extent to which new needs generated new manufacturing methods. The ALCO plants involved were partially torn down, and deep holes dug to accommodate vertical plating and rinsing tanks. After daylong conferences of ALCO engineers searching for the best way of meeting the AEC's exacting specifications, the following process was arrived at:

1.   A huge planer shaved and beveled heavy steel plates to the exact size for welding, after which the plates were formed into pipe under tremendous pressure in a bending roll.

2.   After a submerged-arc welding machine automatically welded the outside seams, flanges were welded to the pipe-ends on rotation positioners. Since these welds were to be subject to the most rigorous leak test ever devised, ALCO used over 100 specially trained welders at this stage of production.

3.   Both end flanges of each pipe were machined simultaneously on what was then one of the world's largest lathes; this allowed machining to extremely close tolerances.

4.   The pipe was immersed in 6 successive cleaning baths, including alkaline rinse, muriatic acid rinse, and sulfuric etch; it was antiseptically clean before entering the nickeling vat. After plating, it got another boiling rinse before the leak test.

Leaks were tested by a mass-spectrometer detecting helium seepage, a test which could find leaks so small it would take a drop of water a century to ease through them.

5.   Each length of pipe was hand cleaned on the inside, sealed with special galvanized dust-tight covers, and finally shipped by rail to the AEC at Oak Ridge, Tennessee.

This project was so successful that ALCO later received an AEC contract to build the first land-based non-experimental nuclear reactor to operate in the United States. Construction and design included a number of "firsts:" first power reactor to use stainless steel-clad fuel elements combined with light water as coolant and moderator, first reactor whose components were air transportable, and the most compact non-experimental reactor built to date. Ground was broken on October 5, 1955, at Fort Belvoir, Virginia; within eighteen months the unit was ready to supply up to 1925 KW of power.

Not only did ALCO design, fabricate, and supervise the field erecting of this reactor, known as the APPR-1, but also ALCO was responsible for the manufacture of some of its most important components: the reactor vessel, the steam generator, the control rod drives, and the pressurizer. When completed, the reactor not only produced power, but served as a training facility for the Army and Navy, giving on-the-job training to future operators of other reactors.

In 1958, ALCO received another AEC contract, this one to design and construct the primary loop for the APPR-1A (later called the SM-1A) reactor for installation in Alaska. 1959 brought still another contract, this one for the first truly "packaged" nuclear plant to be installed at "Camp Century," Greenland. Buried in trenches in the Ice Cap, it demonstrated the feasibility of such an operation.

When an ALCO-built reactor installed at Ft. Greeley, Alaska, finally went "critical," ALCO was the only company in the world to have three nuclear power plants operating at one time. In 1963, ALCO, having developed new production methods, new designs, new shipping methods, and having employed several production testing methods basic to the atomic energy industry, sold its nuclear power engineering department and all existing design and construction contracts to Allis-Chalmers.

ALCO IN THE FIFTIES

The Fifties were an important decade for ALCO; the Company still in name at least a locomotive company, recognized the diversity of its products and exploited that diversity both in the promotion of new technology and in the business market.

ALCO-Dunkirk was a recognized leader in heat exchanger design, performance, and production. ALCO had produced heat exchangers for South America, feed-water heaters for eastern plants, evaporators for refineries, chemical plants, and power plants; it had designed and produced the heat transfer equipment used in the Nation's Butadiene plants (Butadiene is a vital base chemical for manufacturing synthetic rubber), air coolers to cool processed natural gas, and pressure vessels and pipe. A large and marketable business, the Dunkirk heat exchanger business was sold to Worthington Pump Company in 1962. The plant itself was sold to a county development plan corporation. That same year, the Beaumont plant, a related industry, was sold to the Schaffer Tool Co.

ALCO still made diesel engines, of course; in the early fifties ALCO redesigned and refined its Model 244 Diesel engine and came out with the Model 251, which had greater output and reduced maintenance. In 1953, ALCO once again experimented with new fuels and engines; it joined with the Bituminous Coal Research Committee to develop a coal-burning "turbine" for locomotive use.It successfully passed extensive tests at Dunkirk, but the project was abandoned when funding for further work was withdrawn by the Bituminous Coal Research Committee.

In 1953, ALCO's sales reached a new peak of $440,710,000; $85,000,000 of this was for products other than locomotives. These products are an impressive and varied list: combat tanks, heat exchangers, pressure vessels, pipe for petro-chemical and power industries, diesel engines for pipeline pumping, for marine vessels, for municipal power and other stationary applications, oil field drilling and producing equipment, springs and circular forgings, specialized products for the AEC, aircraft engine containers, gas turbine generators, storage tanks, and other special heavy-metal equipment.

THE KOREAN WAR

The only non-motor car company to build tanks, ALCO was praised by the Government for its ordnance record in building the M-47 combat tanks, and was the last civilian producer to end tank production in 1954. ALCO produced over 2,000 M-47 and M-48 tanks for the United States Army.

ALCO worked with the Navy, as well as the Army, participating extensively in heat-transfer equipment for the Navy's nuclear ship pro-

gram—starting with the first nuclear ship, the "Nautilus." Major innovations from this time were the sine-wave exchanger and stainless steel overlay welding.

ALCO moved into sales of its own transportation products on February 13, 1953, when ALCO and General Electric (U.S.A.) agreed not to renew the 1948 agreement to have GE sell ALCO transportation products. ALCO opened its own new sales and service departments in the United States and other areas around the world.

At this time, ALCO diesel locomotives were used on nearly 200 domestic railroads, and by railroads in over 36 foreign countries. The ten millionth horse-power from diesel engines produced by ALCO was delivered to the Missouri Pacific Railroad on May 11, 1954, the end-product of a long line of successively improved diesel engines tested on millions of miles of track throughout the world. ALCO diesel engines had attained the optimum in light-weight design combined with rugged, heavy-duty operations.

In 1955, recognizing its own diversification and choosing to emphasize the changing nature of the Company, the American Locomotive Company changed its name to ALCO Products, Inc. The locomotive business, however, was still expanding; within a year, they had signed a license agreement with Montreal Locomotive Works in Canada and with A. E. Goodwin, Ltd. of Australia.

The next few years saw several important changes in ALCO. Early in 1956, a new line of longitudinal fin tube heat exchangers, called ALCOTWIN, was introduced at the Dunkirk plant. In 1958, ALCO was the leader in obtaining overseas orders for diesel-electric locomotives, attaining a massive 80% of the available market.

Still, ALCO was now ALCO Products, Inc., not just a locomotive company. In 1960, ALCO opened a new cold-wound spring facility at Chicago Heights, and the Forge & Spring Division at Latrobe opened what was then the most modern research and quality control facility in the industry. The cumulative experience of many years in business was branching out in many directions.

ALCO
THE LAST THIRTY YEARS

From the Sixties on, ALCO continued diversifying and improving on old lines, but now ALCO had a new product: itself. With an acknowledged reputation in several fields, and a constant spillover into new fields, the Company itself was sought after by other corporations.

ALCO's locomotive business continued; in 1962, ALCO entered an engine and components license agreement with the Indian Government. ALCO introduced the Century Locomotive during this time—originally three separate models producing 2000, 2400, and 2750 HP respectively. Other models and innovations followed, including the first diesel locomotive tri-mount trucks and the "road switcher" configuration. In 1964, ALCO introduced the first American designed diesel hydraulic freight locomotive. In the same year, two ALCO 16-cylinder engines furnished the power for America's first 5500 HP diesel electric locomotive.

On December 31, 1964, ALCO was purchased by Worthington Corporation, which later merged with Studebaker (1967) to become the Studebaker-Worthington Corporation. After the purchase, ALCO continued innovating, expanding, and diversifying.

In 1965, ALCO produced the first domestic diesel locomotive with an AC/DC transmission, the 3000 HP Century 630. It was the first model with the distinctive aftercooler radiator behind the cab. The following year, ALCO was awarded an engine order by National Steel & Ship Building Company of San Diego for 153 engines, including spares, to be used for propulsion and ship service for 17 U.S. Navy LST's. This was, and still is, the largest single peacetime engine order awarded any U.S. engine builder in ALCO's horsepower range. It was, of course, just one more instance of ALCO's selling a diesel engine for something other than locomotives; ALCO had sold thousands of engines for stationary and marine operations, including mining, U.S. Naval and Merchant Marine vessels, dredging, irrigation, and related installations.

In 1968, ALCO Products, Inc. sold ALCO Forge & Spring, Inc. at Latrobe to the Edgewater Corporation, and retained ALCO Spring Industries at Chicago Heights. ALCO Products, Inc., was now the parent company of five wholly-owned subsidiaries: ALCO Locomotive, Inc. (Schenectady), ALCO Engines, Inc. (Auburn), ALCO Products Service, Inc. (Schenectady), Finserv Computer Corp. (Schenectady) and ALCO Spring Industries (Chicago Heights, Ill.).

1968 also saw the last export diesel locomotive, shipped to F.C. Del Pacifico (Mexico). The last domestic diesel locomotive, a 1000 HP diesel switcher, was delivered out of Schenectady in January of 1969 to Newburgh and South Shore Railroad. That year, ALCO Products, Inc., sold the locomotive design outright to Montreal Locomotive Works, excluding the design rights to the diesel engine.

In the 45 years it produced diesel locomotives, ALCO, its subsidiaries, and its licensees built over 16,000 units which served around the world. This amounted, at that time, to 36,150,000 HP. In its total history, ALCO has produced in excess of 90,000 steam and diesel locomotives.

On February 1, 1970, Studebaker-Worthington, Inc., sold ALCO Engines, Inc., and ALCO Products Service, Inc., to White Motor Corporation. Studebaker-Worthington retained ALCO Products, Inc., ALCO Locomotive, Inc., Finserv Corporation, ALCO Spring Industries, and control of Montreal Locomotive Works-Worthington.

Its locomotive manufacture in Schenectady terminated, ALCO expanded its efforts toward their locomotive licensees and marine and industrial markets. On September 11, 1971, ALCO signed an engine license agreement with UZINEXPORT-IMPORT, Romania. Early in 1972, an engine license was signed with Fiat-Concord of Argentina.

On January 28, 1977, The General Electric Company Limited of London, England, purchased White Industrial Power, Inc. (ALCO), changed its name to ALCO Power, Inc., and retained John V. Sylvester III as the Company's president.

Since that time, many capital improvements in both plant and manufacturing equipment have been made at the Auburn, New York headquarters; millions of dollars more in capital improvements are planned for the future.

ALCO's history is one of men investing time and money in a future they themselves, at times, were not completely sure of—except for a well-founded faith in the potentials of their products, the abilities of their employees, and the tradition of quality in the plants that, over the years, came to make up ALCO. ALCO diesel engines are to be found all over the world at this moment, doing jobs no one could have predicted at the time the Company made the change from steam to diesel engines. (Who would have predicted, in the 1930's, that diesel engines would be used in rocket-launching pads? Who would have guessed their role in the geophysical survey of the ocean floor?) Once again, ALCO is looking for new and broad markets for its present products, and researching the possibilities for future products. The General Electric Company Limited of England has shown the faith in ALCO that investors have always had, and had to their profit. Despite its many varied, useful, often vital products, that faith may be ALCO's most important product.

LIGHTNING

Single-Driver First Passenger Engine
Builder . . . Edward S. Norris Works . . . 1849

ALCO HISTORIC PHOTOS
"LIGHTNING" 1849 First Locomotive Built in Schnectady

Keeseville, Ausable Chasm & Lake Champlain   1 2-4-4T   1898

1837 First steam locomotive produced in the United States. The wood-burning "Sandusky," was built by Rogers Locomotive Works in Paterson, New Jersey, an ALCO predecessor company.

1848 Schenectady Locomotive Engine Manufactory, Schenectady, N.Y., was organized.

1849 First Schenectady locomotive, the "Lightning," was delivered to the Utica & Schenectady Railroad. Weighing 15 tons with 84" drivers, the locomotive sold for $15,800.

1850 In February, the "Lightning," on a run from Utica, N.Y. to Syracuse, N.Y., established a new world record, making the run of 53 miles in 54 minutes.

1851 In May, a new company, The Schenectady Locomotive Works, was formed.

1861-65 Eighty-four steam locomotives were purchased by the U.S. Union Army.

1866 A fire destroyed most of the main building of the plant.

1869 The "Jupiter," built for the Central Pacific Railroad, participated in joining the Transcontinental Railroad at Promontory, Utah, on May 10th.

1876 Locomotive "Number 266" made a run of 81 miles in 82 minutes—the fastest sustained operation recorded up to that time.

1900 On April 30, 1900, Casey Jones and Ol' 382 rode to Glory.

1901 On June 24, The Schenectady Locomotive Works merged with several other companies. They were:

PREDECESSORS WHICH FORMED THE AMERICAN LOCOMOTIVE CO.

Works	Location	Years of Construction		Approx. No. Steam Locomotives Built [1]
Brooks	Dunkirk, N. Y.	1869	1931	4200
Cooke [2]	Paterson, N. J.	1882	1926	3000
Dickson	Scranton, Pa.	1862	1909	1400
Manchester [3]	Manchester, N. H.	1856	1913	1800
Montreal	Montreal, Can.	1904	active	4000
Pittsburgh	Pittsburgh, Pa.	1867	1919	2600
Rhode Island	Providence, R. I.	1866	1907	3400
Richmond	Richmond, Va.	1886	1927	1000
Rogers	Paterson, N. J.	1837	1913	6300
Schenectady	Schenectady, N. Y.	1851	1968	47300 [4]

(1) From THE STEAM LOCOMOTIVE IN AMERICA by A. W. Bruce
(2) Originally Danforth-Cooke, started in 1852
(3) Originally Amoskeag Mfg. Co., started in 1849
(4) Prior to the merger in 1901 6300 locomotives

1904 ALCO bought control of the 2-year-old Locomotive & Machine Co. of Montreal Ltd. (Name later changed to Montreal Locomotive Works, Ltd.)

1905	ALCO purchased the Rogers Locomotive Works, Paterson, N.J., founded in 1837.
1906	The first ALCO Automobile was produced in Providence, R.I., under license from Automobiles M. Berliet of Lyons, France, after an investment of $6,000,000.
1908	ALCO announced that the Berliet License was discontinued and that ALCO would design and manufacture its own automobile.
1909	An ALCO automobile, driven by Henry Fortune Grant, won The Vanderbilt Cup on Long Island, N.Y., with an average speed of 62.81 MPH.
1910	ALCO again won The Vanderbilt Cup. Grant and his "Bete Noire" won the race by 25 seconds with an average speed of 65.18 MPH. The 50,000th steam locomotive, a Pacific Type, was shipped.
1911	Walter P. Chrysler, the works manager for The Allegheny Plant, moved to Detroit to work for Buick Motor Company. The Chrysler Corporation was subsequently founded on June 6, 1924.
1913	ALCO closed its automobile manufacturing facility because it proved to be unprofitable.
1917	ALCO was rated 61st largest company in Forbes.
1924	ALCO produced the first commercially successful diesel electric locomotive (300 HP) for The Central Railroad of New Jersey. The locomotive is now exhibited in the Baltimore & Ohio Railroad Museum in Baltimore, MD.
1926	ALCO purchased The Railway Steel Spring Company of Latrobe, Pa., and Chicago Heights, Illinois.
1928	ALCO built the first diesel-electric passenger locomotive in the U.S.A. using a McIntosh & Seymour Engine. The locomotive developed 900 HP from a V12 diesel and was purchased by The New York Central.
1929	The McIntosh & Seymour Diesel Engine Company, Auburn, N.Y., founded in 1886, was purchased by ALCO.
1930	ALCO designed and manufactured the tunnel shields used for the digging of the Holland and Lincoln Tunnels under the Hudson River, connecting New Jersey and Manhattan. ALCO designed and manufactured its first solid fuel injection engine.
1931	The ALCO 531 (12.5" x 13") engine was produced.
1935	ALCO built the "Hiawatha," the first streamlined locomotive produced in America, for The Chicago, Milwaukee and St. Paul Railroad. It had a sustained speed of 100 MPH and a top speed of 120 MPH.
1936	ALCO developed water-tight doors and windows, controlled from the bridge of passenger ships. This equipment was installed on the liner "America" and others.
1938	ALCO turbo-supercharged the model 531 engine, increasing the horsepower by 100%.

1939	ALCO introduced the first diesel-electric road locomotive.
1940-45	ALCO produced 7,362 army tanks; 3,314 M-7 tank destroyers; 2,300,000 shells; 410,000 fragmentation bombs; 2,574 gun carriages and gun mounts; and 4,488 steam/diesel electric locomotives. Employment went from 5,950 in 1941 to 15,500 in 1945. In 1941, ALCO built the largest locomotive in the world, the "Big Boy," for The Union Pacific Railroad. It weighed, with tender, more than 1,200,000 pounds, had sixteen 68-inch drive wheels, and achieved 7,000 HP.
1944	The all-time annual production peak in steam locomotives was reached when 1,354 were built.
1945	ALCO acquired The Beaumont Iron Works Company, Beaumont, Texas. This company produced oil production equipment.
1948	ALCO produced its 75,000th steam locomotive.
1949	ALCO received a contract from the Atomic Energy Commission (AEC) to produce nickel-plated pipe at the newly-acquired Cincinnati, Ohio, plant and at the Dunkirk, New York, plant.
1950	Thousands of M-47 and M-48 tanks and aircraft engine containers were built for the Korean Police Action Effort.
1953	ALCO joined The Bituminous Coal Research, Inc., to develop a coal-burning "gas turbine" for locomotive use. A prototype was built and tested at Dunkirk, N.Y. The project was abandoned when funding for further work was withdrawn. A new diesel engine, the ALCO 251 (9" x 10.5") was introduced. ALCO participated extensively in heat-transfer equipment for the U.S. Navy's Nuclear Ship Program, beginning with the first nuclear sub "Nautilus." Major innovations were sine-wave exchanger and stainless steel overlay welding.
1955	American Locomotive Company changed its name to ALCO Products, Inc., to emphasize the diversification of products manufactured.
1956	Hi-Qua-Led Steel; Free-Machining, Leaded-Steel Forgings; and Alcotwin, a new line of Longitudinal Fin Tube Heat Exchangers were introduced by the Latrobe, Pa., and Dunkirk, N.Y., plants.
1957	ALCO built the first non-experimental nuclear reactor (APPR-1) to operate in the United States. This reactor is located at Fort Belvoir, Va.
1958	This year, ALCO received 80 percent of the available diesel locomotive overseas market. ALCO received a contract to design and construct the primary loop for the APPR-1A (later called the SM-1A) nuclear reactor for installation in Alaska.
1959	ALCO received a contract to build the first truly "packaged" nuclear plant destined for installation at "Camp Century," Greenland.
1961	The PM-2A (packaged nuclear plant) was installed and put into operation. Buried in trenches in the ice cap, it demonstrated the feasibility of such an operation.

1962   The SM-1A, an ALCO-built reactor, was installed at Fort Greely, Alaska. When this unit went operational, ALCO was the only company in the world to have three of its manufactured nuclear power plants operating at one time.

The heat exchanger and feed water heater business at the Dunkirk, N.Y., plant was sold to Worthington Pump Company. The Beaumont Iron Works, Texas, was sold to the Schaffer Tool Co.

1963   All nuclear contracts were farmed out and/or sold to Baldwin-Lima-Hamilton, Blaw-Knox and Struthers-Wells, and ALCO terminated its involvement in the nuclear field.

The Dunkirk, N.Y., plant was sold to the Dunkirk Development Corp.

The Cincinnati, Ohio, plant was sold to a warehousing company.

1964   The first American-designed diesel hydraulic freight locomotive was introduced by ALCO. Equipped with two ALCO 12-cylinder engines, it was sold to The Southern Pacific Railroad.

Two ALCO 16-cylinder engines furnished the power for America's first 5500 HP diesel-electric locomotive. This unit was sold to The Union Pacific Railroad.

On December 31, 1964, ALCO Products, Inc., was purchased by Worthington Corporation.

1965   ALCO produced the first domestic locomotive with an AC/DC transmission, the 3000 HP Century 630.

1966   ALCO received an order for 153 engines, including spares, for 17 U.S. Navy LST's. To date, this is the largest single peacetime engine order awarded any U.S. engine builder in ALCO's horsepower range.

1967   The Studebaker Corporation merged with Worthington Corporation, forming Studebaker-Worthington, Inc. (SWI). ALCO became a wholly-owned subsidiary.

1968   ALCO sold ALCO Forge & Spring, Inc., Latrobe, Pa., to Edgewater Corp.

The following companies changed from divisions to subsidiaries of ALCO Products, Inc.:

    ALCO Locomotive, Inc., Schenectady, N.Y.

    ALCO Engines, Inc., Auburn, N.Y.

    ALCO Products Service, Inc., Schenectady, N.Y.

    Finserv Computer Corp., Schenectady, N.Y.

    ALCO Spring Industries, Chicago Heights, Ill.

1969   ALCO Products, Inc. terminated domestic locomotive production and sold the locomotive design to the Montreal Locomotive Works. The design rights to the diesel engine were not included.

ALCO delivered two of its first 18-cylinder diesel engines.

1970   On February 1, Studebaker-Worthington, Inc., sold ALCO Engines, Inc. and ALCO Products Service, Inc. to White Motor Corporation effective 6/30/69. White Motor Corporation merged these companies into White Industrial Power, Inc.

1971   White Industrial Power, Inc., received an order for 9 diesel engines (6—V16 and 3—V8) for the 399 foot "Polar Star," the largest U.S. Coast Guard ice breaker ever built.

1973   ALCO celebrated its 125th anniversary by holding an open house at the Auburn, N.Y., facility. A repeat order for 9 engines was placed for the second U.S. Coast Guard's largest series ice breaker, the "Polar Sea."

1976   Three new research and development engine test cells were placed into operation.

1977   On January 28th, the General Electric Company Limited of England purchased White Industrial Power, Inc., and changed the name to ALCO Power Inc.

1979   ALCO received an order for 74 diesel engines for locomotive service in Brazil.

New York Central   6000 4-8-4   1945

Delaware & Hudson   1537 4-6-6-4   1946

STEAM LOCOMOTIVES BY WHEEL ARRANGEMENT REFERENCE

Adirondack & St. Lawrence   St. Lawrence   2-4-6T 1896   67"   55T

Delaware & Hudson Canal Co.   300   2-2-4T 1889   54"

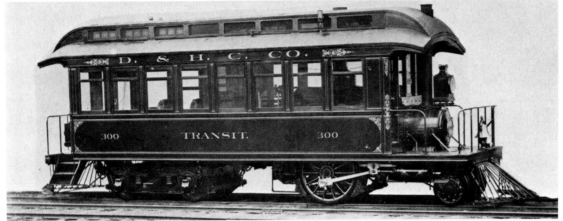

New York Central Lines   24   4-4-0   1905   48T

Rochester & Lake Ontario   31   0-4-4T 1885   43"

Chicago, Rock Island & Pacific (Boiler Press. 250 psi)   2552   1908   38"52T

Delaware, Lackawanna & Western   B   1909

New England   198   1897   42"   58T

New Jersey & New York (Erie)   680   1897   42"

Alco (Dickson) Early Plantation Gauge 3'-0"   —   0-4-0T   24"   7T

Carnegie Steel — Duquesne Works   8   0-4-0T 1895

C.P. & Co. Ltd. — Homestead Works   19   0-4-0T

Dep't. Rys. & Canals — Canada Gauge 3'-0"   2   0-4-0T 1913   30"   14T

Hydro-Electric Power Commission Ontario-Canada   47   0-4-0T 1920   42"   50T

Frank Jones Brewing   1   0-4-0T 1894   40"

Laclede Steel   3   0-4-0T 1923

Lakefield Portland Cement — Canada   3   0-4-0T 1905   33"   28T

Lehigh Valley   3500   0-4-0T 1900

Mackenzie, Mann — Canada   11   0-4-0T 1913   34 1/2"   29T

Oliver Coke & Furnace   2   0-4-0T 1894   26 1/2"   10T

Pittsburgh Plate Glass   5   0-4-0T 1922   36"   33T

Welland Ship Canal Construction — Canada   1   0-4-0T 1928   42"   52T

Ferrocarril del Pacifico — Mexico Gauge 3'-0"   1   0-4-2T 1914   33 1/2"   21T

La Fortunee Estate — Trinidad, B.W.I.   0-4-2T 1920   33 1/2"   23T

El Oro   1   0-4-4T 1898   37"

Atlas Portland Cement   5   2-4-2T   1899   40"   43T

Brazilian Portland Cement   1   2-4-2T   1925

Magma Arizona   Gauge 3'-0"   1   2-4-2T   1915   30 1/2"   23T

Pullman Palace Car Co. Railroad   4   2-4-2T   1893   28"   52T

Sung-Wu Railway — China Gauge 5'-2 1/2"   2   2-4-2T 1897

Dominion Coal — Canada   8   2-4-4T 1900 62"   67T

Flint & Pere Marquette   71 2-4-4T 1883

Boston, Revere Beach & Lynn   Gauge 3'-0"   24 2-4-4T 1914 49 3/5" 46T

Nantucket Railroad   Gauge 3'-0"   2   2-4-4T 1910 40"   25T

New York Central Lines   49 2-4-4T 1910   74T

Wright & Ketcham — T. & H. RR.   3 2-4-4T 1884 37"

Chicago & Northern Pacific   20 4-4-4T 1891 57"   50T

Fort Worth Belt   4   0-4-0   1904   50"   40T-34T

Anticosti Island — Canada   1   2-4-0   1910   36"   22T-15T

Ferrocarril del Pacifico — Mexico Gauge 3'-6"   1   2-4-0   40"   27T-12T

Hawaii Railway   Gauge 3'-0"   3   2-4-2   1901   36"

Boston & Albany   289   4-4-0   1900   75"   68T-48T

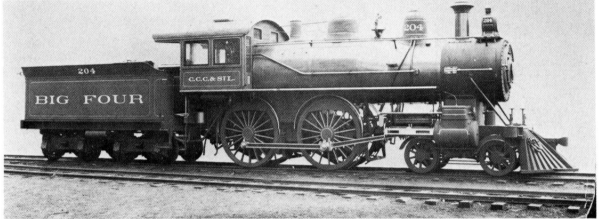

Cleveland, Cincinnati, Chicago & St. Louis   204   4-4-0   1898   78"   65T-51T

Colorado Southern, New Orleans & Pacific   192   4-4-0   1907   69"   67T-54T

Columbia & Puget Sound   18   4-4-0   1910   62"   57T-45T

Maine Central   144   4-4-0   1905   69"   53T-45T

Montpelier & Wells River   13   4-4-0   1912   69"   64T-53T

New York Central Lines — P. & L.E.   329   4-4-0   1906   72"   76T-72T

Seaboard Air Line (Richmond Locomotive)   542   4-4-0   1895

Ann Arbor — (Detroit, Toledo & Tronton)   200   4-4-2   1907   69"   80T-67T

Chesapeake & Ohio   83   4-4-2   1902   72"   87T-60T

Chicago, Indianapolis & Louisville (Monon)   301   4-4-2   1901   73"   83T-56T

Chicago, Milwaukee, St. Paul & Pacific   4   4-4-2   1937   84"   145T-133T

Chicago, Rock Island & Pacific   1013   4-4-2   1905   73"   90T-70T

Chicago, Rock Island & Pacific   1302   4-4-2   1901   78 1/2"   84T-54T

Cleveland, Cincinnati, Chicago & St. Louis   396   4-4-2   1901   78"   87T-58T

Missouri Pacific   1198   4-4-2   1904   79"   97T-59T

Missouri Pacific   5537   4-4-2   1907   78"   98T-73T

New York, New Haven & Hartford   1100   4-4-2   1907   100T-LOCO

Pennsylvania Lines — P.L.W. of P.   7452   4-4-2   1905   80"   100T-70T

Canadian Pacific   3002   4-4-4   1936   80"   132T-99T

British Columbia Mills, Timber & Trading — Canada   6   0-6-0T 1904 42"   36T

Cumberland Railway & Coal — Canada   10 0-6-0T 1904 50"   60T

Leetonia & Cherry Valley — M.A. Hanna   1 0-6-0T 1910 44"   55T

Michigan Northern Power   1 0-6-0T 1929 44"   66T

Newport News Shipbuilding & Dry Dock   5   0-6-0T   1918   46"   60T

Reliance Rock   1   0-6-0T   1925   44"   62T

Cuba Central Railway   154   2-6-2T   1913   50"   57T

Cuban Government Prison Commission Gauge 3'-0"   1   2-6-2T   1927   30 1/2"   32T

District of Columbia Commissioners 1 2-6-2T 1920 41" 44T

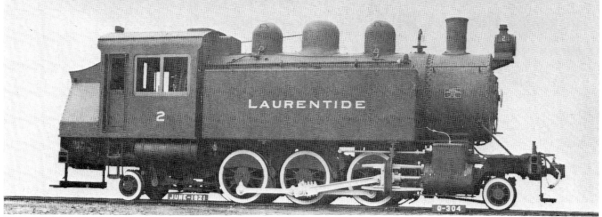

Laurentide — Canada 2 2-6-2T 1921 47" 85T

MacArthur Bros. & Winston 25 2-6-2T 1908 48" 68T

Quincy 2 2-6-2T 1924 44" 60T

Walter A. Woodward Lumber　　　　　　　3　2-6-2T 1927　44"　　66T

Chattanooga Lookout Mountain　　　　　1　2-6-4T 1888

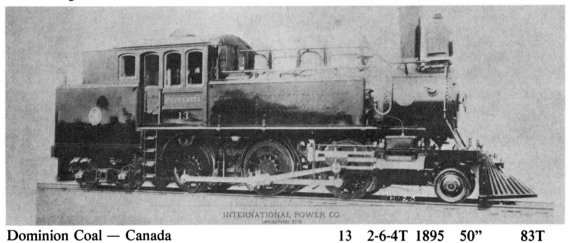

Dominion Coal — Canada　　　　　　　13　2-6-4T 1895　50"　　83T

Jamaica Railway — Jamaica　　　　　　22　2-6-4T 1894　50"

Panama Railroad Gauge 5'-0"   101   2-6-4T 1906   54"   92T

New York Central & Hudson River   829   2-6-6T 1891   64"

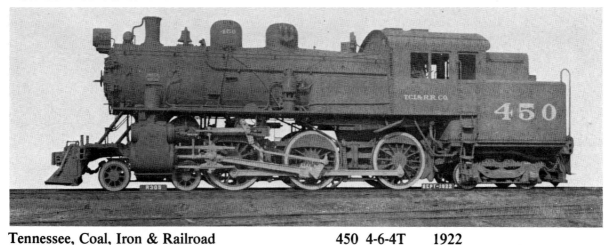

Tennessee, Coal, Iron & Railroad   450 4-6-4T   1922

Boston & Albany — N.Y.C. Lines   400   4-6-6T 1928   176T

Boston & Albany   148   0-6-0   1913   57"   87T-51T

Canadian Copper   2   0-6-0   1895   50"   40T-31T

Chicago & North Western   2047   0-6-0   1914   51"   68T-55T

Columbia & Puget Sound   17   0-6-0   1910   51"   63T-42T

Cornwall Ore Bank (Note the 4-wheeled tender)   7   0-6-0   1918   46"   71T-15T

Delaware, Lackawanna & Western   71   0-6-0   1901   51"   66T-37T

Delaware, Lackawanna & Western   119   0-6-0   1908   51"   66T-40T

Eastern Car — Canada   1   0-6-0   1913   46"   41T-27T

El Paso & South Western   404   0-6-0   1907   51"   75T-44T

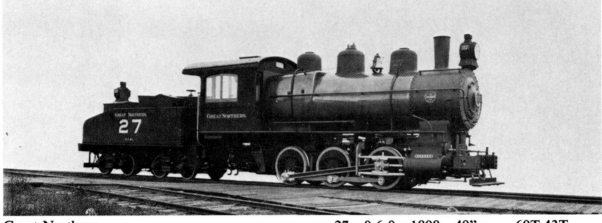

Great Northern   27   0-6-0   1898   49"   69T-43T

Kansas City Southern   99   0-6-0   1905   51"   65T-42T

Missouri, Kansas & Texas   375   0-6-0   1904   57"   73T-55T

New York Central Lines — M.C.-C.S. — Canada 8597 0-6-0 1909 57" 86T-51T

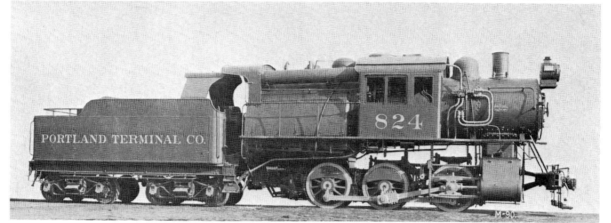

Portland Terminal — (Maine Central) 824 0-6-0 1912 51" 75T-52T

Toronto, Hamilton & Buffalo 41 0-6-0 1906 51" 63T-38T

Canadian Copper Co. 20 2-6-0 1913 50" 78T-51T

Colorado & North Western   Gauge 3'-0"   1   2-6-0   1897   42"   35T-LOCO

Colorado & North Western   Gauge 3'-0"   278   2-6-0   1916   43"   28T-26T

Copper River & North Western   101   2-6-0   1909   57"   68T-52T

Essex Terminal — Canada   8   2-6-0   1918   50"   67T-48T

—50—

Greater Winnipeg Water District — Canada   3   2-6-0   1915   50"   58T-51T

Great Northern   371   2-6-0   1896   55"   65T-43T

Illinois Central   575   2-6-0   1901   56 1/2"   85T-68T

Minneapolis, St. Paul & Sault Ste. Marie — (Soo Line) 109   2-6-0   1903   55"   74T-58T

New York, Chicago & St. Louis   85   2-6-0   1890   63"   50T-30T

Nickel Range Railway — Canada   1   2-6-0   1907   50"   65T-50T

Pennsylvania   869   2-6-0

Pere Marquette   217   2-6-0   1901   56"   70T-47T

Quebec Railway, Light, Heat & Power — Canada 22 2-6-0 1928 56" 61T-37T

Roberval & Saguenay — Canada 13 2-6-0 1927 50" 83T-55T

Vandalia Line 158 2-6-0 1906 63" 94T-73T

Wabash 758 2-6-0 1899 63" 65T-49T

Alabama Great Southern   440   4-6-0   1900   69"   72T-48T

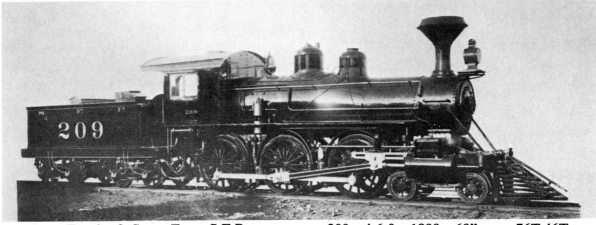

Atchison, Topeka & Santa Fe — S.F.P.   209   4-6-0   1899   69"   76T-46T

Bangor & Aroostook   92   4-6-0   1911   62"   80T-53T

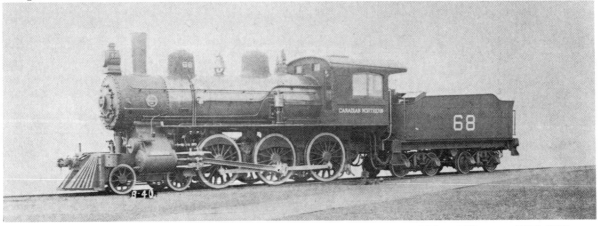

Canadian Northern   68   4-6-0   1903   63"   70T-49T

Canadian Northern   206   4-6-0   1904   63"   80T-59T

Canadian Pacific   656   4-6-0   1906   63"   96T-63T

Canadian Pacific   860   4-6-0   1903   69"   82T-61T

Canadian Pacific   1085   4-6-0   1912   63"   100T-68T

Canadian Pacific   1313 4-6-0 1903

Canadian Pacific   2473 4-6-0 1908 62" 71T-53T

Canadian Pacific   2747 4-6-0 1908

Central New England   300 4-6-0 1909 69" 81T-60T

Chicago & Alton   240   4-6-0   1893   64"   66T-40T

Chicago & North Western   160   4-6-0   1891   63"   78T-47T

Chicago & North Western   341   4-6-0   1899

Chicago Great Western   173   4-6-0   1901

Chicago, Indianapolis & Louisville — (Monon)　　120　4-6-0　1900　69"　79T-48T

Chicago, Rock Island & Pacific　　840　4-6-0　1896　57 3/8"　74T-40T

Colorado & Southern　　323　4-6-0　1903　67"　85T-57T

Columbus & Cincinnati Midland　　10　4-6-0　1885　55"　49T-35T

Delaware & Hudson   502   4-6-0   1903

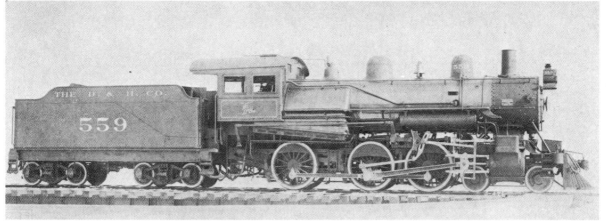

Delaware & Hudson   559   4-6-0   1907

Delaware, Lackawanna & Western   1052   4-6-0   1907

Denver & Rio Grande   734   4-6-0   1899   63"   84T-60T

Erie   771 4-6-0 1896 62"   72T-44T

Evansville & Terre Haute   552 4-6-0 1905 63"   89T-63T

Florence & Cripple Creek-Golden Circle Gauge 3'-0"   52 4-6-0 1899 42"   41T-27T

Florida East Coast   30 4-6-0 1900 63"   57T-40T

Fort Smith & Western 9 4-6-0 1903 63" 72T-LOCO

Georgia, Southern & Florida 138 4-6-0 1900 56" 75T-LOCO

Grand Trunk — Canada 999 4-6-0 1905 72" 82T-56T

Grand Trunk — Canada 1014 4-6-0 1906 72" 82T-66T

Grand Trunk Pacific 618 4-6-0 1907 63" 82T-68T

Great Northern of Canada 63 4-6-0 1901

Great Northern 668 4-6-0 1893

Gulf, Beaumont & Kansas City 13 4-6-0 1900

Gulf Coast Lines   72   4-6-0   1921   95T-LOCO

Illinois Central   1   4-6-0   1898   63"   82T-52T

Indiana & Illinois Southern   40   4-6-0   56"   61T-38T

International & Great Northern   250   4-6-0   1908   62"   85T-68T

Jamestown, Chautauqua & Lake Erie   11   4-6-0   1901

Long Island   138   4-6-0   1913   92T-LOCO

Maine Central   368   4-6-0   1906   63"   87T-55T

Michigan Central — C.S.   459   4-6-0   1900   63"   77T-51T

Michigan Central — N.Y.C.   8272   4-6-0   1905   63"   80T-53T

Missouri Pacific   1107   4-6-0   1901   68"   73T-47T

New York Central & Hudson River   948   4-6-0   1897

New York Central Lines — B&A   1916   4-6-0   1907   104T-LOCO

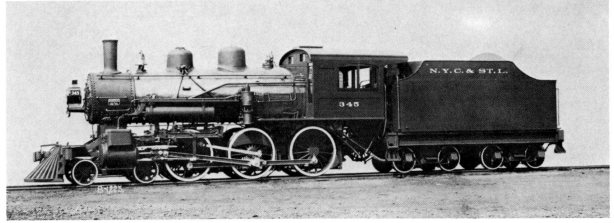

New York, Chicago & St. Louis   345   4-6-0   1910   62"   72T-62T

Oahu Railway & Land Co. - Hawaii Gauge 3'-0"   88   4-6-0   1916

Oregon Short Line — UP   754   4-6-0   1898   57"   86T-50T

Pere Marquette   158   4-6-0   1902   62"   68T-51T

Phoenix & Eastern   14   4-6-0   1903   63"   71T-25T

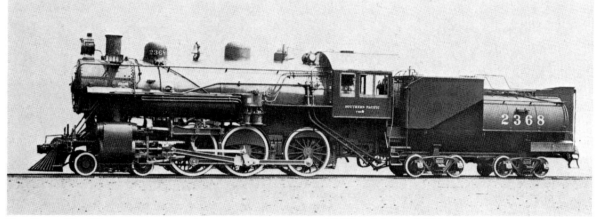

St. Louis & San Francisco   719   4-6-0   1906   63"   96T-64T

Southern Pacific   2368   4-6-0   1913

Toronto, Hamilton & Buffalo   30   4-6-0   1908   60"   76T-51T

Union Pacific 1703 4-6-0 1899 57" 85T-53T

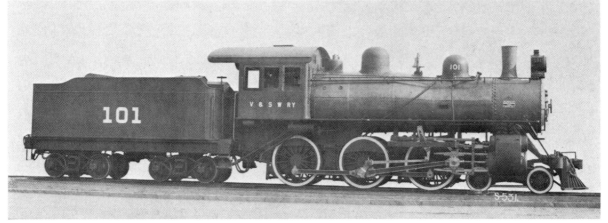

Virginia & South Western 101 4-6-0 1907 63" 80T-61T

Virginian — (Tidewater Railway) 203 4-6-0 1907 63" 94T-74T

Western Ry. of Alabama — (Atlanta & West Point) 129 4-6-0 1911 61" 95T-68T

Cathels & Sorenson — Canada   1   2-6-2   1923   44"   63T-44T

J.H. Chambers   2   2-6-2   1925   44"   63T-40T

Chicago, Burlington & Quincy   2118   2-6-2   1906   69"   109T-74T

Chicago Great Western   264   2-6-2   1902

Chicago, Milwaukee, St. Paul & Pacific-C.M.&P.S.   2134   2-6-2   1909   63"   104T-78T

Colorado Springs & Cripple Creek Dist. Gauge 3'-0"   101   2-6-2   1900

Lake Whatcom Logging   1   2-6-2   1909   48"   67T-37T

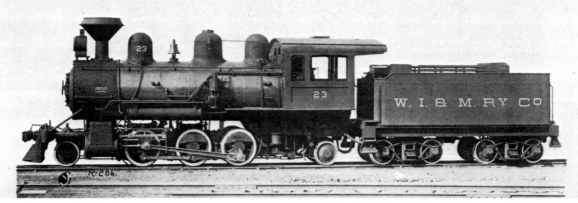

Washington, Idaho & Montana   23   2-6-2   1910   43"   59T-43T

Delaware & Hudson   608   4-6-2   1914   69"   147T-83T

Illinois Central   1071   4-6-2   1911   125T-LOCO

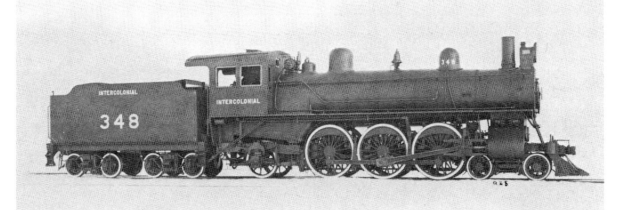

Intercolonial Railway — Canada   348   4-6-2   1905   72"   97T-60T

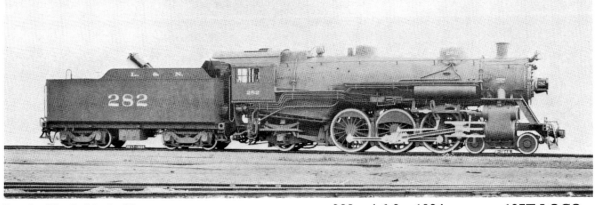

Louisville & Nashville   282   4-6-2   1924   127T-LOCO

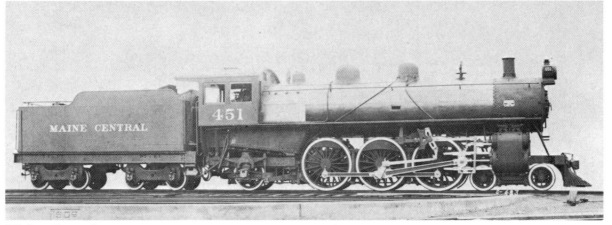

Maine Central 451 4-6-2 1907

Mexicano — Mexican Railway Co. 134 4-6-2 1938 69" 126T-65T

Minneapolis & St. Louis 500 4-6-2 1920

Missouri Pacific 6000 4-6-2 1925

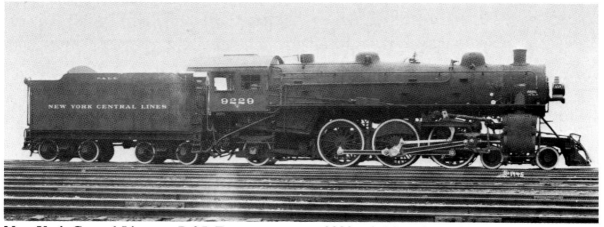

New York Central Lines — P.&L.E.   9229   4-6-2   1917   72"   138T-75T

Northern Pacific   310   4-6-2   1905   69"   110T-71T

Oregon Railroad & Navigation — (UP)   190   4-6-2   1904   77"   107T-67T

Pennsylvania   3395   4-6-2   1911   159T-LOCO

Pennsylvania Lines West of Pittsburgh   7049   4-6-2   1912   80"   144T-75T

Rutland   82   4-6-2   1925   69"   139T-98T

Southern   1212   4-6-2   1904   72"   110T-63T

Southern   6479   4-6-2   1926

Southern Pacific   2400   4-6-2   1904   111T-LOCO

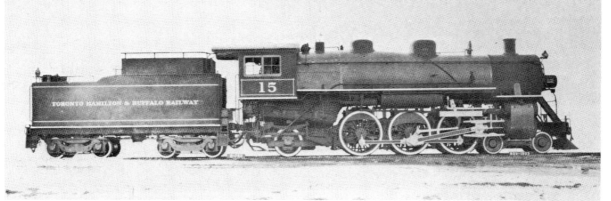

Toronto, Hamilton & Buffalo   15   4-6-2   1923   69"   132T-77T

Union Pacific   170   4-6-2   1912   139T-LOCO

New York Central Lines — B&A   601   4-6-4   1928   75"   177T-102T

Canadian Pacific   2815   4-6-4   1930   75"   176T-150T

Canadian Pacific (Royal Hudson)   2862   4-6-4   1940

Chicago & North Western   4002   4-6-4   1938   206T-LOCO

Chicago, Milwaukee, St. Paul & Pacific   100   4-6-4   1938   84"   208T-188T

National Railways of Mexico   2703   4-6-4   1937   73"   146T-87T

New York Central   5445   4-6-4   1938   79"   183T-158T

New York Central Lines — C.C.C.&St.L.   6603   4-6-4   1929   79"   176T-152T

New York, Chicago & St. Louis — (Nickel Plate)   173   4-6-4   1927   73"   159T-104T

Bauxite & Northern (American Bauxite Co.)   2   0-8-0T 1915   46"   66T

Deep River Logging   9   2-8-2T 1925

Kanawha & Michigan   556   2-8-2T 1902   120T

Long-Bell Lumber   800   2-8-2T 1925

Nevada Northern   5   2-8-2T 1906   111T

Sugar Pine Lumber   1   2-8-2T 1923   44"   94T

Togoland Military Railway Gauge 39-3/8"-Meter   30   2-8-2T 1917   38"   48T

Dominion Coal — Canada   14   2-8-4T 1896   50"   208T

Bessemer & Lake Erie   253 0-8-0 1936   **140T-LOCO**

Canadian National   8364 0-8-0 1929 51"   **109T-74T**

Central New England   13 0-8-0 1922 51"   **110T-81T**

Central Railroad of New Jersey   273 0-8-0 1912 56"   **115T-78T**

Central Railroad of New Jersey   304   0-8-0   1923   119T-LOCO

Detroit Terminal   15   0-8-0   1916   58"   120T-74T

New York Central Lines — L.S.&M.S.   4299   0-8-0   1913   58"   120T-74T

Temiskaming & Northern Ontario — Canada   155   0-8-0   1920   53"   104T-67T

Algoma Central & Hudson Bay — Canada   37   2-8-0   1908   56"   98T-65T

Arizona & Swansea   3   2-8-0   1910   50"   67T-46T

Baltimore & Ohio   2635   2-8-0   1906   60"   105T-69T

Bangor & Aroostook   176   2-8-0   1914   56"   104T-73T

Boston & Albany   1052   2-8-0   1913   63"   121T-72T

Canadian Northern — Canadian Government   2489   2-8-0   1918   63"   121T-78T

Canadian Pacific   673   2-8-0   1898   51"   73T-43T

Canadian Pacific   767   2-8-0   1900   57"   75T-50T

Canadian Pacific   1205   2-8-0   1901   57"   80T-57T

Canadian Pacific   1888   2-8-0   1908   63"   111T-71T

Castle Valley   102   2-8-0   1910   50"   80T-53T

Central of Georgia   1013   2-8-0   1901   55"   94T-59T

Central Mexicano   199 2-8-0 1897 57"   90T-45T

Charlotte Harbor & Northern   50 2-8-0 1913 54"   82T-67T

Chesapeake & Ohio   355 2-8-0 1903

Chesapeake & Ohio   525 2-8-0 1904 56"   93T-60T

Chicago, Terre Haute & Southeastern   680 2-8-0 1912 61"   122T-75T

Coal Belt (Peabody Coal)   2 2-8-0 1904 50"   69T-54T

Colorado & Southern   475 2-8-0 1902 57"   96T-69T

Columbia & Puget Sound   16 2-8-0 1910 52"   70T-39T

Copper Range   30   2-8-0   1907   50"   85T-50T

Denver, North Western & Pacific   112   2-8-0   1910   55"   110T-75T

Duluth, South Shore & Atlantic   91   2-8-0   1924   51"   96T-61T

Duluth, Winnipeg & Pacific   2906   2-8-0   1917   63"   120T-79T

Elgin, Joliet & Eastern   79   2-8-0   1899   51"   83T-51T

Erie   1401   2-8-0   1899   57"   85T-66T

Grand Trunk — Canada   663   2-8-0   1906   63"   103T-72T

Great Northern   450   2-8-0   1892   55"   69T-42T

Kansas City Southern   483   2-8-0   1906

Louisville & Nashville   891   2-8-0   1898   55"   78T-44T

Midland Terminal   2   2-8-0   1896   52"   75T-44T

Minneapolis, St. Paul & Sault Ste. Marie — (Soo Line)   433   2-8-0   1902   55"   89T-57T

Monongahela   145   2-8-0   1916   51"   100T-81T

National Railways of Mexico Gauge 3'-0"   300   2-8-0   1936   41"   59T-45T

National Railways of Mexico   791   2-8-0   1921   55"   88T-77T

Nevada Northern   95   2-8-0   1914   51"   98T-73T

New York Central Lines — M.C.   7826   2-8-0   1909   63"   118T-76T

New York, Chicago & St. Louis   151   2-8-0   1906   62"   84T-62T

Pacific Great Eastern — P. Welch — Canada   51   2-8-0   1913   57"   88T-68T

Pennsylvania Southern   5   2-8-0   1911   57"   80T-51T

Pere Marquette 344 2-8-0 1901 56" 82T-55T

Pittsburgh, Bessemer & Lake Erie 81 2-8-0 1899 54" 86T-47T

Rio Grande Western 1198 2-8-0 1906 57" 108T-76T

St. Louis & San Francisco 1280 2-8-0 1907 57" 103T-75T

St. Louis, Iron Mountain & Southern   1857   2-8-0   1901   55"   84T-52T

San Antonio, Uvalde & Gulf   23   2-8-0   1913   54"   73T-62T

Silver City & Northern   2   2-8-0   1892

Southern   231   2-8-0   1896   56"   70T-47T

Texas Central   127   2-8-0   1910   51"   73T-51T

Toronto, Hamilton & Buffalo   53   2-8-0   1909   55"   102T-68T

Union Pacific   1316   2-8-0   1898

Western Pacific   34   2-8-0   1909

Alton & Southern   16   2-8-2   1937   135T-LOCO

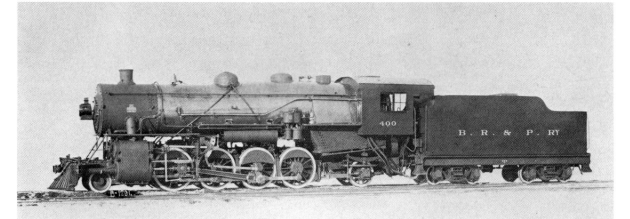

Ann Arbor   187   2-8-2   1923

Buffalo, Rochester & Pittsburgh   400   2-8-2   1912   63"   140T-85T

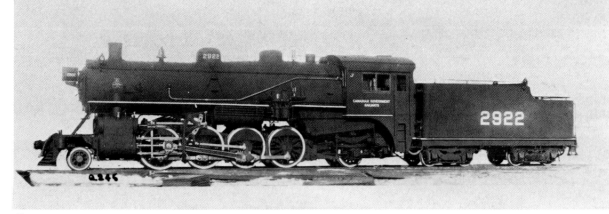

Canadian Government Railways   2922   2-8-2   1917   63"   141T-86T

Canadian National   3533   2-8-2   1923   158T-LOCO

Canadian Pacific   5440   2-8-2   1944   63"   169T-100T

Chicago & Eastern Illinois   1918   2-8-2   1912   63"   150T-86T

Grand Trunk — Canada   500   2-8-2   1913   142T-LOCO

Louisville & Nashville   1999   2-8-2   1924   127T-LOCO

Missouri, Kansas & Texas   802   2-8-2   1915   157T-LOCO

Missouri Pacific Lines   1115   2-8-2   1926

National Railways of Mexico   919   2-8-2   1921   57"   132T-83T

Newfoundland Railway — Canada Gauge 3'-6"   1001   2-8-2   1930   48"   73T-52T

New York Central Lines — L.S.&M.S.   4008   2-8-2   1912-3   156T-LOCO

New York, New Haven & Hartford   3008   2-8-2   1916   126T-LOCO

Northern Pacific   1743   2-8-2   1913   160T-LOCO

St. Louis & Ohio River   2   2-8-2   1928   55"   137T-95T

Seaboard Air Line   303   2-8-2   1914   63"   141T-92T

Sierra   36   2-8-2   1930   104T-LOCO

Southern   4856   2-8-2   1924

Union Pacific   717   2-8-2   1912   63"   143T-86T

Western Pacific   335   2-8-2   1929   166T-LOCO

Chesapeake & Ohio   2730   2-8-4   1943-4   230T-LOCO

Chicago & North Western   2806   2-8-4   1927   63"   199T-144T

Missouri Pacific Lines   1125   2-8-4   1928   63"   202T-143T

New York Central System — P.&L.E.   9401   2-8-4   1947

New York, Chicago & St. Louis (Nickel Plate)   703   2-8-4   1934

Toronto, Hamilton & Buffalo   202   2-8-4   1928   192T-LOCO

Wheeling & Lake Erie   6401   2-8-4   1937   69"   204T-182T

Central Pacific   2012   4-8-0   1895

Central Railroad of New Jersey   429   4-8-0   1899

Central Railroad of Pennsylvania   4   4-8-0   1893

Chicago & Eastern Illinois   173   4-8-0   1900

Delaware & Hudson (Boiler Pressure 500psi)   1403   4-8-0   1933   63"   191T-137T

Great Northern   103   4-8-0   1898

Illinois Central   640   4-8-0   1899

Norfolk & Western   1094   4-8-0   1907

Northern Pacific   3   4-8-0   1897

Southern Pacific of California   2026   4-8-0   1898

Bangor & Aroostook   100   4-8-2   1929   62"   152T-91T

Chesapeake & Ohio (U.S. RR. Administration)   133   4-8-2   1918   69"   176T-97T

Chicago, Rock Island & Pacific   4060   4-8-2   1929

Florida East Coast   412   4-8-2   1924   73"   157T-101T

Minneapolis, St. Paul & Sault Ste. Marie - (Soo Line) 4000   4-8-2   1926

Missouri Pacific   5337   4-8-2   1927   73"   197T-137T

New York Central   3000   4-8-2   1940

New York Central Lines — C.C.C.&St.L.   6225   4-8-2   1929   69"   184T-155T

Rutland   93   4-8-2   1946   174T-LOCO

Tennessee Central   552   4-8-2   1926   63"   137T-84T

Union Pacific   7000   4-8-2   1922   73"   173T-119T

Brazilian National Railways Gauge 39 3/8" Meter 1001   4-8-4   1945   59"   108T-85T

Canadian National   6205   4-8-4   1942   73"   200T-139T

Chicago, Rock Island & Pacific　　　　5100　4-8-4　1944　74"　　234T-151T

Delaware & Hudson　　　　308　4-8-4　1943　75"　　235T-150T

Delaware, Lackawanna & Western　　　1631　4-8-4　1934　74"　　224T-157T

Grand Trunk Western　　　　6300　4-8-4　1927　73"　　200T-134T

Lehigh Valley   **5220   4-8-4   1931   70"   211T-179T**

Nashville, Chattanooga & St. Louis   **566   4-8-4   1930   70"   197T-97T**

National Railways of Mexico   **3027   4-8-4   1946   70"   194T-121T**

New York Central   **800   4-8-4   1931   69"   218T-156T**

New York Central   5500   4-8-4   1946   79"   243T-161T

New York Central   6000   4-8-4   1945   75"   236T-169T

Timken Roller Bearing Co. — (Later N.P. 2626)   1111   4-8-4   1930   73"   209T-147T

Toledo, Peoria & Western   80   4-8-4   1937   69"   180T-162T

Union Pacific 806   4-8-4   1937   77"   233T-183T

Union Pacific 825   4-8-4   1939   80"   242T-203T

Union Pacific 841   4-8-4   1944   246T-LOCO

Burlington & Missouri River 275   0-10-0   1891

ALCO U.S.A. Export (U.S.S.R.) 1080 2-10-0 1917 100T-LOCO

Boston & Maine 3006 2-10-2 1920 61" 179T-103T

Canadian National 4026 2-10-2 1920 57" 160T-100T

Chicago, Indianapolis & Louisville (Monon) 600 2-10-2 1914 57" 170T-89T

Illinois Central   2601   2-10-2   1916   184T-LOCO

Pennsylvania Lines   7227   2-10-2   1919   218T-LOCO

Texas & Pacific   540   2-10-2   1919   166T-LOCO

Union Pacific   5044   2-10-2   1923   63"   190T-110T

Bessemer & Lake Erie   625   2-10-4 1937   260T-LOCO

Canadian Pacific   5922   2-10-4 1938   63"   224T-141T

Central Railway of Brazil   Gauge 39 3/8"   1666   2-10-4 1940   48 1/4"   119T-58T

Central Vermont   702   2-10-4 1928   60"   210T-135T

Southern Pacific Lines 5043 4-10-2 1927 63 1/2" 223T-146T

Union Pacific 8800 4-10-2 1926

Sorocabana Railway — Brazil 1019 4-10-2 1940

Union Pacific 9054 4-12-2 1929 67" 249T-156T

Denver, North Western & Pacific   200   0-6-6-0 1908   164T-LOCO

Kansas City Southern   710   0-6-6-0 1912   156T-LOCO

New York Central & Hudson River   1300   0-6-6-0 1913   51"   174T-79T

West Side Belt   1000   0-6-6-0 1910   55"   163T-77T

Denver & Salt Lake   210   2-6-6-0 1913   180T-LOCO

Eastern Railway — France   6001   2-6-6-0 1908   164T-LOCO

Natal Government — South Africa   Gauge 3'-6"   337   2-6-6-0 1910   45 1/2"   104T-51T

Virginian   500   2-6-6-0 1909

Buffalo, Rochester & Pittsburgh   745   2-6-6-2 1923   57"   223T-103T

Central of Georgia   1908   2-6-6-2   1913

Chesapeake & Ohio   701   2-6-6-2   1914   56 1/4"   214T-86T

Chicago & Alton   701   2-6-6-2   1910   62"   164T-86T

Chicago, Milwaukee & St. Paul (C.M.St.P.&P.)   5026 2-6-6-2 1912   198T-LOCO

Mogyana Railway — Brazil Gauge 39 3/8" Meter   754 2-6-6-2 1920   45"   93T-47T

National Railways of Mexico Gauge 3'-0"   242 2-6-6-2 1929   43"   102T-52T

National Railways of Mexico   2035 2-6-6-2 1937   57"   197T-97T

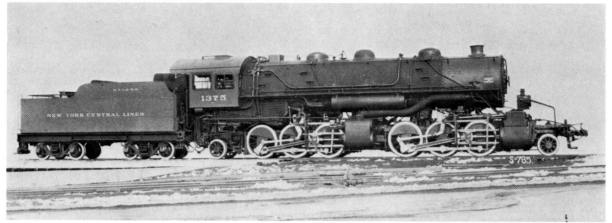

New York Central & Hudson River   1375   2-6-6-2   1911   57"   177T-77T

Norfolk & Western   1308   2-6-6-2   1912   56"   203T-79T

Verde Tunnel & Smelter   500   2-6-6-2   1920   224T-LOCO

Western Pacific   204   2-6-6-2   1917   214T-LOCO

Wheeling & Lake Erie   804 2-6-6-2 1917 63" 218T-88T

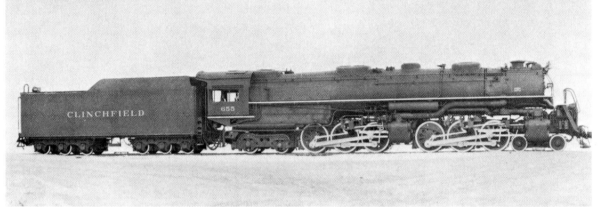

Clinchfield   655 4-6-6-4 1943 304T-LOCO

Delaware & Hudson   1505 4-6-6-4 1940 69" 299T-155T

Denver & Rio Grande Western   3800 4-6-6-4 1943 313T-LOCO

Northern Pacific   5107 4-6-6-4 1936 69"   312T-200T

Northern Pacific   5138 4-6-6-4 1943   322T-LOCO

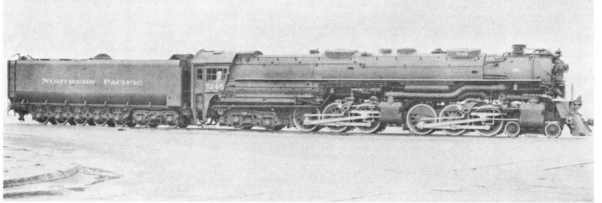

Northern Pacific   5148 4-6-6-4 1944 70"   322T-175T

Spokane, Portland & Seattle   900 4-6-6-4 1937 69"   311T-197T

Spokane, Portland & Seattle   911 4-6-6-4 1944 70"   319T-176T

Union Pacific   3938 4-6-6-4 1937 69"   291T-156T

Union Pacific   3977 4-6-6-4 1943   313T-LOCO

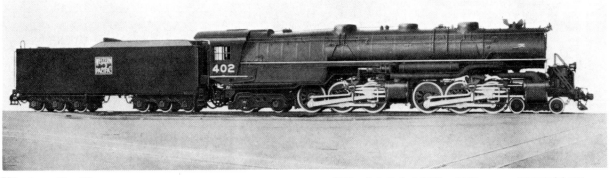

Western Pacific   402 4-6-6-4 1938 70"   295T-201T

Baltimore & Ohio   2401 0-8-8-0 1911   232T-LOCO

Bingham & Garfield   100 0-8-8-0 1911 51"   229T-84T

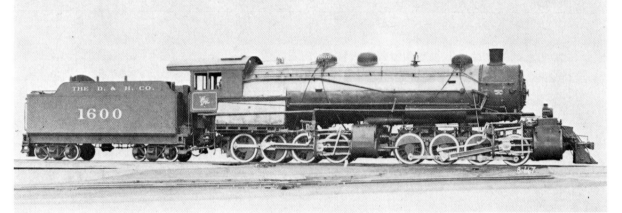

Delaware & Hudson   1600 0-8-8-0 1910   223T-LOCO

Erie   2600 0-8-8-0 1907   205T-LOCO

New York Central Lines — P.&L.E.   9091 0-8-8-0 1916   232T-LOCO

Norfolk & Western   990 0-8-8-0 1910 56"   188T-79T

Baltimore & Ohio   7208 2-8-8-0 1916   247T-LOCO

Kansas City Southern   754 2-8-8-0 1918 57"   248T-100T

Union Pacific   3617 2-8-8-0 1920   247T-LOCO

Buffalo, Rochester & Pittsburgh 801 2-8-8-2 1918   283T-LOCO

Chesapeake & Ohio   1119 2-8-8-2 1924   298T-LOCO

Clinchfield   741 2-8-8-2 1924   272T-LOCO

Denver & Rio Grande   1075   2-8-8-2   1912

Denver & Rio Grande Western   3608   2-8-8-2   1927   63"   325T-172T

Interstate   21   2-8-8-2   1923

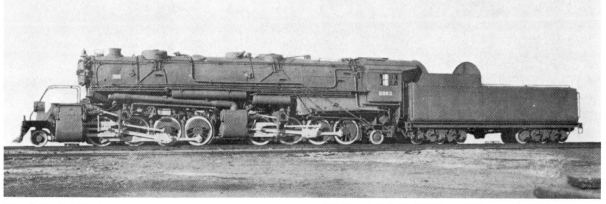

Norfolk & Western   2063   2-8-8-2   1923   57"   269T-133T

Northern Pacific   4008 2-8-8-2 1913

Paulista Railway — Brazil   90 2-8-8-2 1913   113T-LOCO

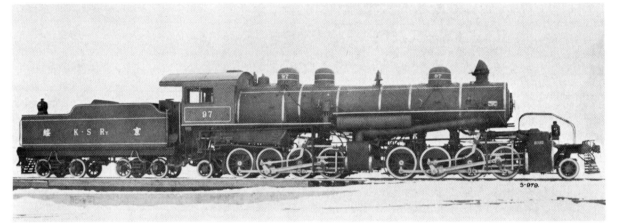

Pekin-Kalgan — China   97 2-8-8-2 1914 50"   145T-63T

Pennsylvania   3396 2-8-8-2 1911 56"   242T-93T

St. Louis & San Francisco   2007   2-8-8-2   1910   57"   209T-75T

Seaboard Air Line   515   2-8-8-2   1918

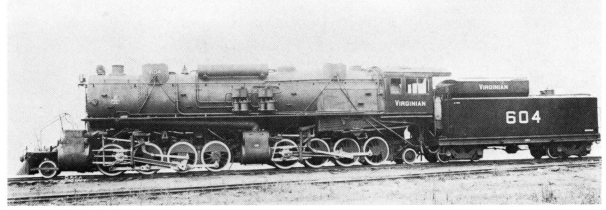

Virginian   604   2-8-8-2   1912

Virginian   900   2-8-8-2   1919   266T-LOCO

Northern Pacific 5000 2-8-8-4 1928-9 359T-LOCO

Union Pacific 4002 4-8-8-4 1941 68" 381T-171T

Union Pacific 4022 4-8-8-4 1944 68" 386T-174T

Virginian 802 2-10-10-2 1918 56" 342T-107T

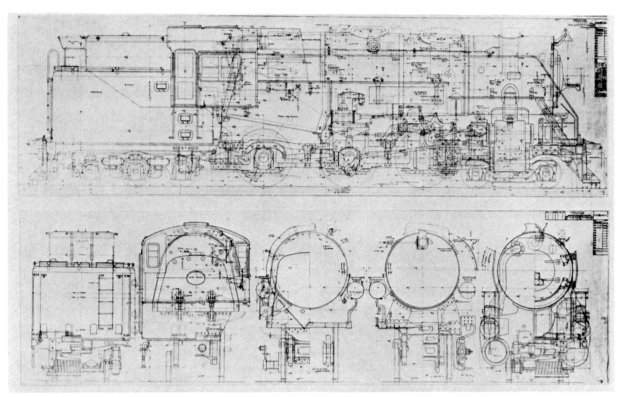

Boston & Albany (N.Y.C.)   400 4-6-6T   1928

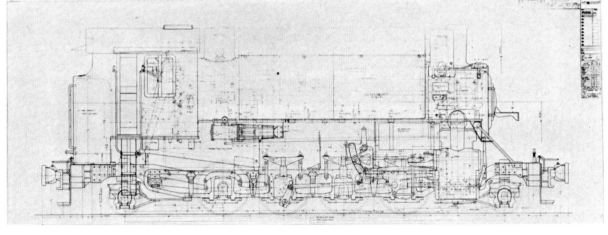

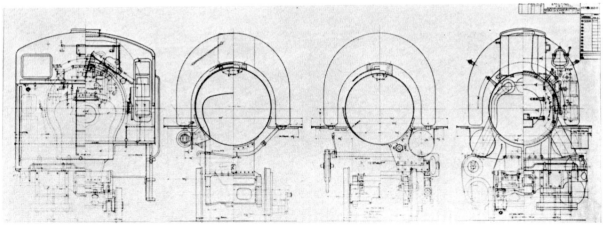

Crossett Western Co   10 2-8-2T   1929

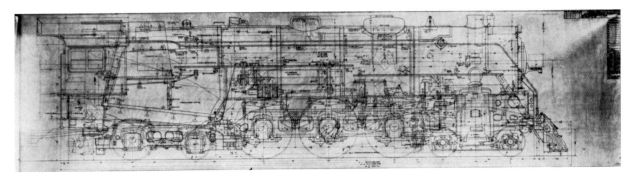

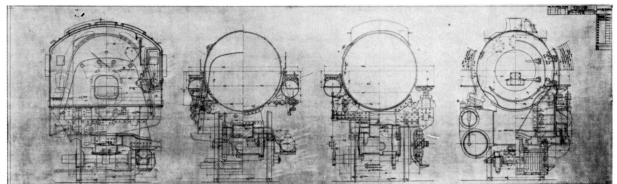

Boston & Albany (N.Y.C.)   605 4-6-4   1930

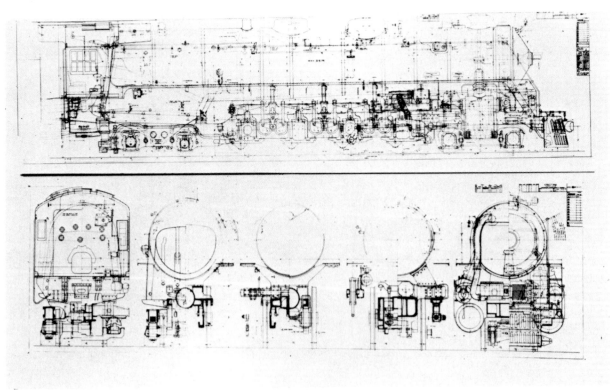

New York Central   5500 4-8-4   1946

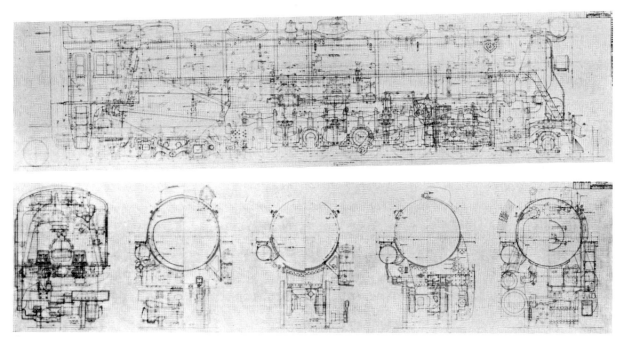

Central of Vermont 700 2-10-4 1928

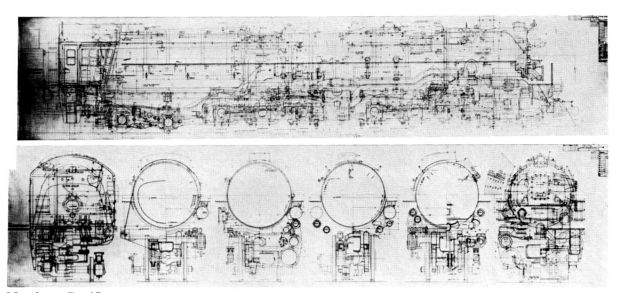

Northern Pacific 5142 4-6-6-4 1944

Aroostook Valley   53 B-B   1912   36"   41T 400HP

Bush Terminal   10 B-B   1907   36"   41T 640HP

Butte, Anaconda & Pacific (with Tractor No. 3)   48 B-B-B   1914   46"   122T 1650HP

Woodward Iron   27 B-B   1911   33"   35T 200HP

Chicago, Milwaukee & St. Paul   10203 A&B 2-B-B+B-B-2 1915-6

Great Northern   5002 B-B   1908-9

Great Northern   5011 1-C-C-1 1927   259T

Interborough — New York Elevated Railway   1544 B-B

Mexicano (Mexican Railway)   1001 B-B-B   1923   46" 155T 2520HP

New York Central   1155 B-B-B-B 1913

New York Central (Units 1 & 2)   1201 B-B-B-B 1926 44" 175T 3320HP

New York Central & Hudson River   3237 2-D-2   1908-9

New York Central & Hudson River   6000 1-D-1   1904   113T 1700HP

New York Central Lines — DRT   7500 B-B   1908

New York, New Haven & Hartford   18 1-C-C-1 1908

New York, New Haven & Hartford   068 2-B-B-2 1912

New York, New Haven & Hartford 0112 1-B-B-1 1926 42" 140T 1350HP

New York, New Haven & Hartford 0217 B-B   1926 42" 100T 1760HP

Norfolk & Western   2515 2 (1-B-B-1) 1924 62" 414T 4750HP

Virginian   100 3(1-B-B-1) 1925 62" 638T 7125HP

DIESEL ENGINES

America's first road-passenger and road-freight diesel-electric locomotives were ALCO-built in 1928 for the New York Central System — a railroad that at that time was perhaps the most innovative and progressive in terms of motive-power. The first early diesel engines supplied for ALCO diesel locomotives from Ingersoll-Rand, were of 300HP size, for yard switcher application. This arrangement lasted for about five years until ALCO purchased a successful diesel engine builder, McIntosh & Seymour of Auburn, N.Y. McIntosh & Seymour eventually built a four-stroke 12½" x 13" cylinder size diesel engine, which with an option, offered a Buchi turbocharger almost doubling the horsepower output. Referred to as the "539 Series", these diesel engines ranged from 600-1000HP (with turbocharging) for railway applications, which was for yard switching, except for a few mainline road passenger units called the DL109 Model, which had two 1,000hp diesel engines installed per unit. The "539 Series" became so successful in yard switcher service that over the years ALCO held a commanding share of the yard switcher market in North America. In 1940, ALCO entered into an agreement with General Electric Company, in which the former would be supplied generators, traction motors and controls for diesel-electric locomotives from the latter.

At cessation of World War II hostilities in 1945, ALCO understood the coming demand for quantity deliveries of both road-passenger and road-freight diesel-electric locomotives in North America, and knew that the steam locomotive market was almost dried-up. Responding early to the challenge for a suitable higher horsepower road diesel engine for these new locomotives in the 1500-2000HP range size, ALCO created the "244 Series" diesel engine, a four-stroke 9" x 10½" cylinder size diesel engine. Converting the huge Schenectady steam locomotive facilities was a major accomplishment and was completed in 1948 — an ALCO milestone. Meanwhile, the "244 Series" diesel-engines were moderately successful, and ALCO was determined to improve and perfect their operation. Refinements and modifications were incorporated into improvements, including greater internal engine lubricating capacity, and as a result, in the early 1950's, ALCO offered the "251 Series" diesel engine to the locomotive market. This new engine was well-received and is currently in production at ALCO POWER, Inc.'s Auburn, N.Y. plant, for 800-4000HP locomotives, power generation and marine power applications.

Illustrations of ALCO diesel-electric locomotive production over the years start with the early units up to 1940 — a turning-point in diesel-electric locomotive production designs from ALCO. This year began the introduction of a new line of switcher locomotives and a line of streamlined road units. As a result, after 1940 production, locomotive illustrations appear by yard switcher units, S1, S3, S2 and S4 followed by road-switchers RS1, RS2 and RS3 models and variations of these road switchers. This is then followed by DL109 Model cab and booster units, followed by streamlined road freight and passenger designs. Directly after come the cab and booster units of the PA streamlined road passenger designs perhaps the greatest carbody-streamline styling ever conceived for the railways. Right after this, into the mid-nineteen fifties, we have examples of ALCO PRODUCTS, INC.'s higher horsepower diesel-electric road switchers of various designs. This is followed by ALCO's famous Century Series diesel-electric locomotives, introduced in 1963, until cessation of locomotive production in 1969. Especially included was a representative collection of Montreal built diesel-electric locomotives in retrospect showing the "ALCO designs" in Canada by MLW up to the current locomotive production of Bombardier, Inc., for World markets, including the Continent's most powerful single-engine diesel-electric locomotive, the M640 Model, of 4000HP. Within the model sub-order groups of illustrations the following caption data is included: railway by alphabetical order, road number, builder's model, year built, driving wheel diameter in inches, weight loaded in tons and horsepower. Shown for some passenger units is maximum speed in mph.

ALCO   300 B-B   1931 38" 64T 300HP

Delaware, Lackawanna & Western   3001 B-B   1926 38" 66T 300HP

Donner Steel   21 B-B   1928 38" 67T 300HP

Erie   20 B-B   1926 38" 67T 300HP

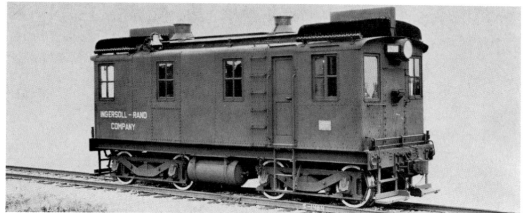

Ingersoll-Rand — B-B 1924 36" 64T 300HP

Ingersoll-Rand 90 B-B 1926 38" 67T 300HP

Jay Street Connecting 300 B-B 1931 38" 64T 300HP

Reading 50 B-B 1926 64T 600HP

American Rolling Mill ARMCO Steel   E101 B-B   1928 38" 108T 600HP

Great Northern   5100 B-B   1926 38" 108T 600HP

Red River Lumber   502 B-B   1926 38" 107T 600HP

Long Island   401 B-B   1925 38" 102T 600HP

Long Island   402 B-B   1928 40" 107T   600HP

New York Central   1500 2-D-2   1928

ALCO   304 B-B   1932   36"57T 300HP

Chiriqui Land — Panama   Gauge 3'-0"   12 B-B   1937   36"   57T 300HP

Delaware, Lackawanna & Western 403 B-B 1933 40" 102T 60

Lehigh Valley 103 B-B 1931 38" 66T 300HP

U.S. Naval Department 4 B-B 1934 36" 57T 300HP

ALCO 600 B-B 1931 40" 100T 600HP

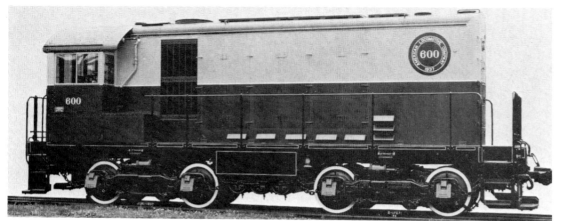

ALCO   600 B-B   1937 40" 99T 300HP

ALCO   601 B-B   1932 40" 101T 600HP

ALCO — Built for Stock   901 B-B   1938 40" 130T 900HP

Atchison, Topeka & Santa Fe   2316 B-B   1939 40" 130T 1000HP

Atlantic Coast Line   1900 B-B   1939 40" 100T   660HP

Boston & Maine   1101 B-B   1938 40" 99T   600HP

Southern Pacific Lines   1002 B-B   1939 40" 99T   660HP

Youngstown & Northern   211 B-B   1937 40" 117T   900HP

Long Island   404 S1   1946 40" 99T   660HP

New York Central   687 S1   1941 40" 107T 660HP

Pennsylvania   9100 S1   1949 40"   660HP

River Terminal   52 S1   1941 40" 100T 660HP

New York Central   880 S3   1950 40"   660HP

Pennsylvania   8879 S3   1951 40"   660HP

Southern Pacific   1023 S3   1951 40"   98T   660HP

Bingham & Garfield   800 S2   1942 40" 115T 1000HP

Canadian Pacific   7010 S2   1943 40" 115T 1000HP

Chicago, Burlington & Quincy   9300 S2   1943 40" 115T 1000HP

Delaware & Hudson   3000 S2   1944 40" 115T 1000HP

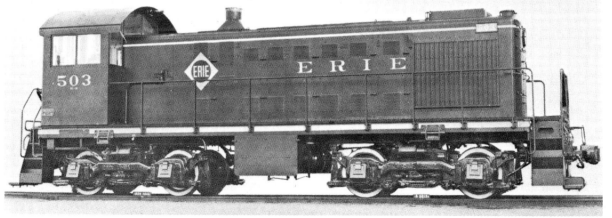

Erie   503 S2   1946 40" 115T 1000HP

National Railways of Mexico   5500 S2   1944 40" 115T 1000HP

New York Central   780 S2   1943 40" 115T 1000HP

Pennsylvania   9282 S2   1949 40" 115T 1000HP

Illinois Northern   31 S4   1950 40" 115T 1000HP

Pennsylvania 8900 S4 1951 40" 1000HP

Southern Pacific 1466 S4 1951 40" 1000HP

Alaska 1000 RS1 1944 40" 1000HP

Central Railway of Brazil Gauge 5'-3" 3112 RS1 1945 40" 121T 1000HP

Chicago, Milwaukee, St. Paul & Pacific   1678 RS1   1941 40"   1000HP

Great Northern   183 RS1   1944 40" 119T 1000HP

Gulf, Mobile & Ohio   1123 RS1   1949 40" 122T 1000HP

Kansas City Southern   1113 RS1   1943 40" 119T 1000HP

Pennsylvania   5639 RS1   1950 40"   1000HP

Spokane, Portland & Seattle   50 RS1   1945 40" 119T 1000HP

Canadian Pacific   8400 RS2   1949 40" 122T 1500HP

Chicago, Indianapolis & Louisville — (Monon)   21 RS2   1947 40" 122T 1500HP

Delaware & Hudson   4003 RS2   1946 40" 115T 1500HP

Elgin, Joliet & Eastern   800 RS2   1948 40" 125T 1500HP

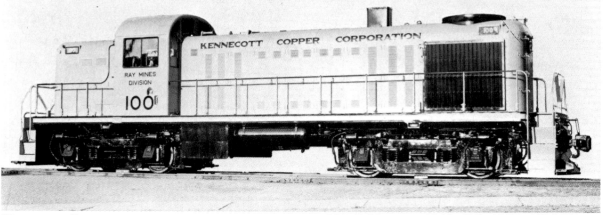

Kennecott Copper   100 RS2   1948 40" 125T 1500HP

Maine Central   553 RS2   1949 40" 115T 1500HP

New York Central   8205 RS2   1949 40" 123T 1500HP

Roberval & Saguenay — Canada   19 RS2   1947 40" 115T 1500HP

Spokane, Portland & Seattle   60 RS2   1949 40" 115T 1500HP

Texas Pacific — Missouri Pacific Terminal   21 RS2   1948 40" 125T 1500HP

Union RR — U.S.Steel   607 RS2   1948 40" 125T 1500HP

Chicago, Milwaukee, St. Paul & Pacific   2487 RS3   1954 40"   1600HP

Great Northern   198 RS3   1950 40" 124T 1600HP

Missouri-Illinois   65 RS3   1953 40" 123T 1600HP

New York Central   8328 RS3 1952 40" 1600HP

Pennsylvania   8440 RS3 1953 40" 1600HP

Piedmont & Northern   101 RS3 1950 40" 1600HP

Reading   497 RS3 1952 40" 1600HP

Spokane, Portland & Seattle   69 RS3   1951 40" 123T 1600HP

National of Mexico   5602 RSD1 1946 40" 127T 1000HP

Sao Paulo Railway — Brazil   500 RSC1 1946 40" 126T 1000HP

U.S. War Dep't. Gauge 5'-0"   8605 RSD1 1944 40" 129T 1000HP

United States Army   B2043 MRS1   1000HP

Chicago, Milwaukee, St. Paul & Pacific   976 RSC2   1946 40" 125T 1500HP

Soo Line   368 RSC2   1949 40"   1500HP

Portuguese Railways   1103 RSC2   1948 40" 119T 1500PH

Union Pacific   DS1187 RSC2   1948 40" 118T 1500HP

Kennecott Copper   201 RSD4   1951 40"   1600HP

Utah Railway   300 RSD4   1952 40" 1600HP

Pennsylvania   8446 RSD5   1952 40"   1600HP

Atchison, Topeka & Santa Fe 120mph   50 DL109   1941 41" 162T 2000HP

Atchison, Topeka & Santa Fe 120mph   50A DL110   1941 41" 165T 2000HP

Chicago & North Western   5007A DL109   1941   2000HP

Chicago, Milwaukee, St. Paul & Pacific   14 DL109   1941   2000HP

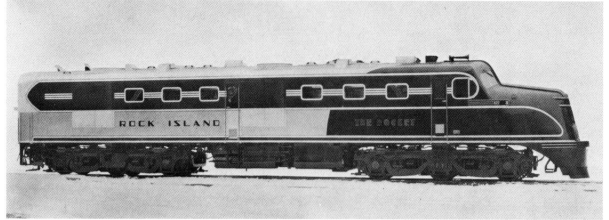

Chicago, Rock Island & Pacific   120mph   622 DL109   1940 40" 163T 2000HP

Chicago, Rock Island & Pacific   120mph   624 DL109   1939 40" 173T 2000HP

Gulf, Mobile & Ohio   120mph   270 DL109   1940 40" 159T 2000HP

New York, New Haven & Hartford   0701 DL109   1941 40" 173T 2000HP

New York, New Haven & Hartford   0752 DL109   1945 40"   2000HP

Southern   120mph   6400-6401 DL109 & 110   1941 40" 326T 4000HP

Southern   120mph   6400-B DL110 1941 40" 163T 2000HP

Southern   120mph   6401 DL109   1941 40" 163T 2000HP

Ann Arbor   52-52A FA2   1950 40"   1600HP

Baltimore & Ohio   801 801X 801A FA,FB.FA 1950 40" 370T 4800HP

Canadian Pacific   4001 FA1   1949 40"   1500HP

Canadian Pacific   4400 FB1   1949 40" 113T 1500HP

Central Railway of Brazil   Gauge 5'-0"   3211 FA   1948 40" 120T 1500HP

Chicago, Rock Island & Pacific   147 FA   1948 40" 116T 1500HP

Chicago, Rock Island & Pacific   147B FB   1948 40" 113T 1500HP

Erie   725 FA   1947 40"   1500HP

Erie   725B FB   1947 40" 115T 1500HP

Great Northern   442 FA   1949 40" 1500HP

Great Northern   442B FB   1949 40" 115T 1500HP

Green Bay & Western   503,507 2(FA) 1949 40" 223T 3000HP

Gulf, Mobile & Ohio   724 FA   1946 40" 114T 1500HP

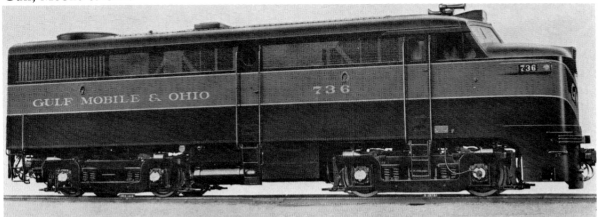

Gulf, Mobile & Ohio   736 FA   1946 40" 114T 1500HP

Gulf, Mobile & Ohio   FB5 FB   1946 40" 112T 1500HP

Kewaunee, Green Bay & Western   501 FA   1947 40" 116T 1500HP

Lehigh Valley   542 FB   1948 40" 118T 1500HP

Lehigh Valley   531 FB   1948 40" 114T 1500HP

Louisville & Nashville   355-356 2(FA2)   1952 40"   3200HP

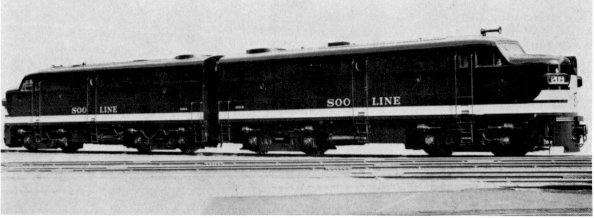

Minneapolis, St. Paul & Sault Ste. Marie   209A&B 2(FA)   1948 40" 238T 3000HP

Missouri-Kansas-Texas Lines   327A&C 2(FA)   1948 40" 238T 3000HP

Missouri Pacific   347-348 2(FA2)   1951   3200HP

National Railways of Mexico   6527A&B FPA FPB 1951 40" 241T 3200HP

New York Central   1000 FA   1947 40" 115T 1500HP

New York Central   2300 FB   1947 40" 112T 1500HP

New York, New Haven & Hartford   0400 FA1   1947 40"   1500HP

New York, New Haven & Hartford   0450 FB   1947 40" 112T 1500HP

New York, New Haven & Hartford   465 FB2   1951 40"   1600HP

Northern Railway of Cuba — (Norte)   1653 FA2   40"   1600HP

Pacifico del Mexico   903 FPA2   1954 40"   1600HP

Pennsylvania   9603 FA   1948 40" 122T 1500HP

Pennsylvania   9603B FB   1948 40" 118T 1500HP

Reading   302 A&B 303 B&A FA FB FB FA 1948 40" 471T 6000HP

St. Louis & San Francisco   5202 FA   1948 40" 117T 1500HP

St. Louis & San Francisco   5301 FB   1948 40" 113T 1500HP

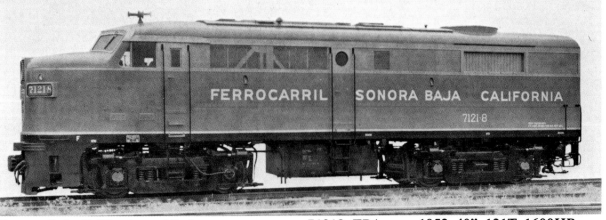

Sonora Baja California — Mexico   71218 FPA   1952 40" 121T 1600HP

Spokane, Portland & Seattle   851 A1,A2 2(FA)   1948 40" 232" 3000HP

Tennessee Central   801 & 801B FA FB   1949 40" 232T 3000HP

Union Pacific   1506A FA   1947 40" 121T 1500HP

Union Pacific   1531B FB   1947 40" 118T 1500HP

Wabash   1200A FA   1949 40" 1500HP

Wabash   1200B FB   1949 40" 1500HP

Western Maryland   301-302 2(FA)   1951 40" 3200HP

Atchison, Topeka & Santa Fe   100mph   51&A&B PA PB PA 1946 42" 475T 6000HP

Denver & Rio Grande Western   600 PA   1947 42" 153T 2000HP

Denver & Rio Grande Western   PB   1947 42" 153T 2000HP

Erie   850 PA   1949 42"   2000HP

Gulf, Mobile & Ohio   291 PA   1946 42" 153T 2000HP

Lehigh Valley   607 608 2(PA)   1948 42" 308T 4000HP

Missouri-Kansas-Texas   151A PA   1949 42" 153T 2000HP

Missouri-Kansas-Texas   157&C 2(PA)   1951 42"   4500HP

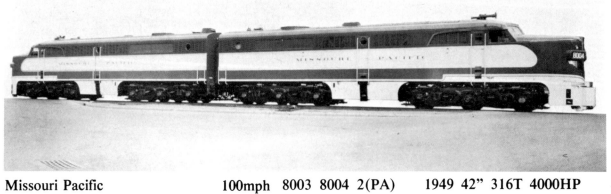

Missouri Pacific   100mph 8003 8004 2(PA)   1949 42" 316T 4000HP

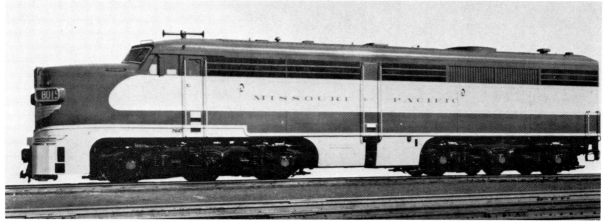

Missouri Pacific   8019 PA   1951 42"   2250HP

New York Central   100mph   4202 PA   1948 42" 155T 2000HP

New York Central — P.&L.E.   4213 PA   1952 42" 157T 2250HP

New York Central   100mph   4302 PB   1948 42" 155T 2000HP

New York, Chicago & St. Louis (Nickel Plate) 185-186 2(PA)   1947 42" 154T 4000HP

New York, New Haven & Hartford   0775 PA   1949 42" 155T 2000HP

Paulista Railway of Brazil   900 PA   1953 42"   2250HP

Pennsylvania   100mph   5750 PA   1947 42" 156T 2000HP

Pennsylvania 100mph 5752B PB 1947 42" 153T 2000HP

St. Louis — Southwestern 300-301 2(PA) 1949 42" 157T 4000HP

Southern 6901 PA 1953 42" 156T 2250HP

Southern Pacific 200 2(PA) 1949 42" 157T 4000HP

Southern Pacific   6023 PA   1952 42" 160T 2250HP

Southern Pacific   6005B PB   1948 42" 155T 2000HP

Union Pacific   996A PA   1947 42" 2000HP

Union Pacific   104mph   998B PB   1947 42" 155T 2000HP

Wabash   1020&A 2(PA)   1949 42" 4000HP

American Freedom Train — Spirit of 1776   1776 PA   1947 2000HP

ALCO Demonstrator   DL600 —   1954 40" 180T 2250HP

Oliver Iron Mining Co. (Cow & Calf)   1218 SSAB9 Model 1956 1800HP

Pennsylvania RR   8617 RS11   1956 1800HP

ALCO Demonstrator   640-1-2-3 RS27   1959 2400HP

416 RS27   1962 2400HP

National of Mexico   7402 RSD12   1959 1800HP

Atchison, Topeka & Santa Fe   800 RSD15   1958 2400HP

Portland Terminal (Oregon)   46 T6   1968 1000HP

ALCO Demonstrator   415 C415   1966 1500HP

Louisville & Nashville   1301 C420   1964 2000HP

New York, Chicago & St. Louis (NPR)   578 C420   1963 2000HP

Green Bay & Western   311 C424   1963 2400HP

Reading Lines   5201 C424   1963 2400HP

Pennsylvania RR   2421 C425   1964 2500HP

ALCO Demonstrator   430-1 C430   1967 3000HP

ALCO Demonstrator   628-4 C628   1964 2750HP

Atlantic Coast Line   2000 C628   1963 2750HP

Delaware & Hudson   605 C628   1963 2750HP

Atlantic Coast Line   2011 C630   1965 3000HP

Southern Pacific   7805 C630   1966 3000HP

Union Pacific

2908 C630 1965 3000HP

Illinois Central 1100 C636 1968 3600HP

Spokane, Portland & Seattle 335 C636 1968 3600HP

Southern Pacific (Diesel-Hydraulic) (2 Engines)   9019 DH643   1963 4300HP

Union Pacific   (2 Engines)   61 C855   1963 5500HP

Greece — Export Model   A-321 DL543   1966 2000HP

Peru — Export Model   614 DL560D   1966 3000HP

Canadian Pacific   7077 S2   1948 1000HP

Canadian Arsenals Limited   1 S3   1952 660HP

Alma & Jonquieres Railway   101 S4   1949 1000HP

Pacific Great Eastern Ry. (BCR)   1003 S13   1959 1000HP

Canadian National   9414 & 9429   FA & FB   1951   3200HP

Canadian National   9442 FA2   1953 1600HP

Canadian National 6765 FPA4 1958 1800HP

Canadian National 6865 FPB4 1958 1800HP

Canadian Pacific   4048 FA2   1951 1600HP

Canadian Pacific   4082 & 4463   FA & FB   1953   3200HP

Canadian National   1732 RSC13   1957 1000HP

Canadian National   1802 RSC24   1959 1400HP

Quebec North Shore & Labrador   102   RS3   1951   1600HP

Canadian National   1822 RS3   1954 1600HP

Canadian National   3074 RS10   1956 1600HP

Canadian Pacific   8581 RS10   1956 1600HP

Ontario Northland Railway   1400 RS10   1955 1600HP

Wabush Lake Railway   909 RS18   1965 1800HP

Canadian National   3224 C424   1967 2400HP

Canadian Pacific   8300 C424   1963 2400HP

Canadian National 2001 C630 1967 3000HP

Canadian Pacific 4507 C630 1968 3000HP

Pacific Great Eastern Ry. (BCR) 702 C630 1969 3000HP

British Columbia Railway 722 M630 1972 3000HP

Canadian National   2300 M636   1970 3600HP

Quebec Cartier Railway   72 M636   1972 3600HP

Canadian Pacific　　　　　　　　　　　　**4744 M640**　　　　**1971 4000HP**

Bombardier (LRC Locomotive)　　　　　　　　　**— LRC**　　　　**1971 2900HP**

British Columbia Railway   642 M420   1973 2000HP

British Columbia Railway   723 M630   1973 3000HP

British Columbia Railway   687 M420B   1975 2000HP

Canadian National   2542 M420   1974 2000HP

Providence & Worcester (U.S.A.)　　　　2001 M420　　　1974 2000HP

Alcan (Roberval & Saguenay)　　　　26 M420TR　　1971 2000HP

Argentina   (Gauge 5'-6")   5574 DL500C   1957 1800HP

Argentina   (Gauge 5'-6")   6480 DL535M   1963 1200HP

Australia   4001 E1662A   1951 1600HP

Bangladesh Bombardier-built   (Meter Gauge 39 3/8")   2412 DL535A   1978 1200HP

Greece   A-458 MX627   1974 2700HP

Jamaica Bombardier-built   132 DL532B   1976   950HP

National of Mexico   5620 RS1   1954 1000HP

National of Mexico   6531-A FB2   1954 1600HP

National of Mexico   7234 RS11   1963 1800HP

National of Mexico   8604 M630   1972 3000HP

Ferrocarril del Pacifico — Mexico   654 M636   1972 3600HP

Nigeria   (Gauge 3'-6")   1720 MX615   1972 1500HP

Peru   616 DL560D   1974 3000HP

Venezuela Bombardier-built   M-001 M420   1976 2000HP

White Pass & Yukon Railway (Gauge 3'-0")   102 DL535E   1969 1200HP

Yugoslavia   665-002 MX626   1972 2600HP

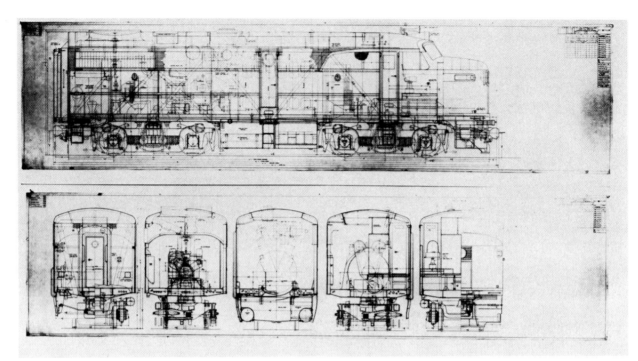

American Locomotive Co.   — FA MODEL 1945 1500HP

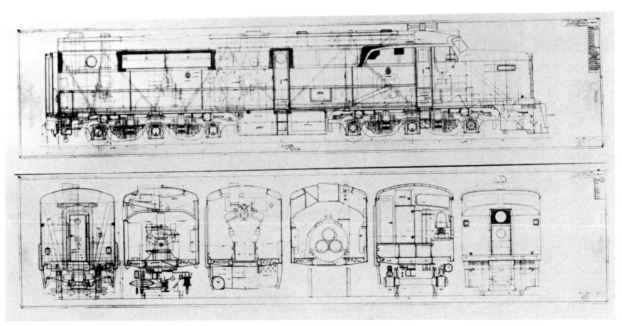

Atchison, Topeka & Santa Fe   51 PA MODEL 1946 2000HP

DL-718-D

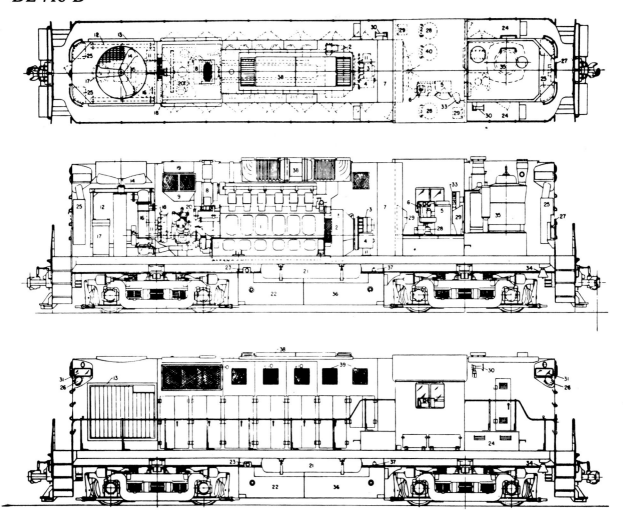

1. Engine	15. Radiator Fan Clutch	29. Cab Heater
2. Main Generator	16. Lubricating Oil Cooler	30. Horn
3. Exciter	17. Lubricating Oil Filters	31. Number Box
4. Auxiliary Generator	18. Lubricating Oil Strainer	32. Headlight
5. Control Stand	19. Engine Water Tank	33. Gauge Panel
6. Brakes Valves	20. Air Compressor	34. Bell
7. Control Compartment	21. Main Air Reservoir	35. Steam Generator
8. Turbosupercharger	22. Fuel Tank	36. Water Tank
9. Turbosupercharger Filters	23. Fuel Tank Filling Connection	37. Water Filling Conn.
10. Air Filters	24. Batteries	38. Dynamic Brake Grids and)
11. Traction Motor Blowers	25. Sand Box	Blower)
12. Radiators	26. Sand Box Cover	39. Air Filters (with Dynamic)
13. Radiator Shutters	27. Hand Brake	Brake)
14. Radiator Fan	28. Cab Seat	40. Cab Seat)

Century 630

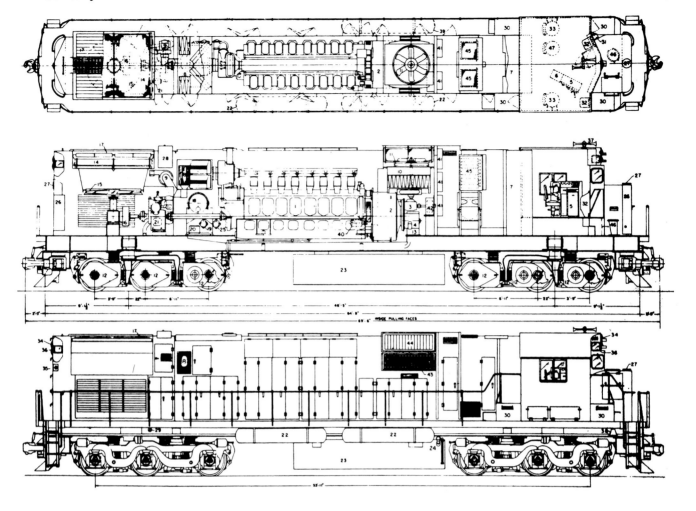

1. Engine	12. Traction Motor	27. Sand Box Fill
2. Main Generator	13. Traction Motor Blower	28. Engine Water Expansion Tank
3. Exciter	14. Radiator	29. Engine Water Fill and Drain
4. Auxiliary Generator	15. Radiator Fan	30. Batteries
5. Control Stand	16. Radiator Fan Clutch	31. Hand Brake
6. Brake Valves	17. Radiator Shutter	32. Cab Heater
7. Control Compartment	18. Lubricating Oil Filter	33. Cab Seat
8. Mechanical Air Cleaner (Engine Air)	19. Lubricating Oil Strainer	34. Headlight
9. Air Cleaner Exhauster	20. Lubricating Oil Cooler	35. Classification Light
10. Mechanical Air Cleaner (Gen. Compartment Air Filtering System)	21. Air Compressor	36. Number Light
	22. Main Air Reservoir	37. Horn
	23. Fuel Tank	38. Bell
11. Fan (Gen. Compartment Air Filtering System)	24. Fuel Tank Filling Connection	39. Dynamic Brake Resistors)
	25. Fuel Oil Filter	40. Toilet) Mods.
	26. Sand Box	41. Cab Seat)

Century 420

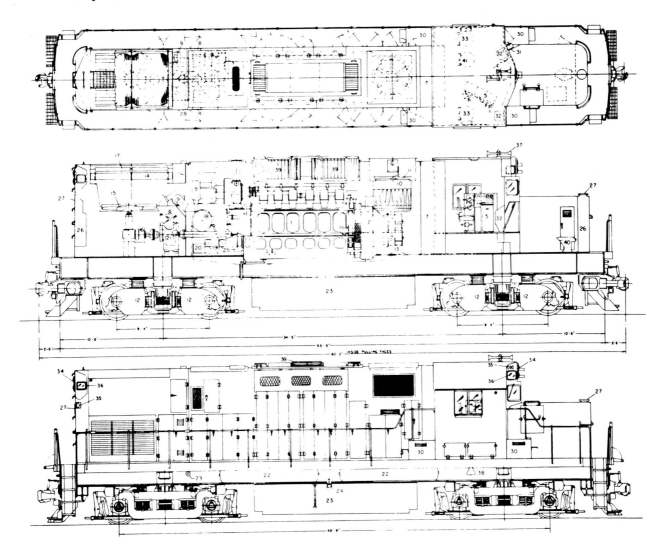

1. Engine
2. Main Generator (Alternator)
3. Gear Box-Fan Drive
4. Auxiliary Generator (Alternator)
5. Control Stand
6. Brake Valves
7. Control Compartment
8. Mechanical Air Cleaner (Engine Air)
9. Air Cleaner Exhauster
10. Mechanical Air Cleaner (Gen. Compartment Air Filtering System)
11. Fan (Gen. Compartment Air Filtering System)
12. Traction Motor
13. Traction Motor Blower
14. Radiator
15. Radiator Fan
16. Radiator Fan Clutch
17. Radiator Shutter
18. Lubricating Oil Filter
19. Lubricating Oil Strainer
20. Lubricating Oil Cooler
21. Air Compressor
22. Main Air Reservoir
23. Fuel Tank
24. Fuel Tank Filling Connection
25. Fuel Oil Filter
26. Sand Box
27. Sand Box Fill
28. Engine Water Expansion Tank
29. Engine Water Fill and Drain
30. Batteries
31. Hand Brake
32. Cab Heater
33. Cab Seat
34. Headlight
35. Classification Light
36. Number Light
37. Horn
38. Bell
39. Starting Air Reservoir
40. Starting Air Motor
41. Main Rectifier
42. Rectifier Air Blower
43. Shutters
44. Radiator and Shutters (Aftercooler)
45. Dynamic Brake Resistors)
46. Toilet   ) Mods.
47. Cab Seat   )